馆藏撷珍

深圳中国钢结构博物馆
馆藏精品图录

|第一辑|

深圳中国钢结构博物馆　编

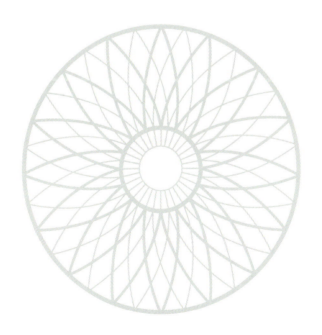

文物出版社

图书在版编目(CIP)数据

馆藏撷珍 ：深圳中国钢结构博物馆馆藏精品图录.
第一辑 / 深圳中国钢结构博物馆编. -- 北京 ：文物出
版社，2020.8
ISBN 978-7-5010-6749-7

Ⅰ. ①馆… Ⅱ. ①深… Ⅲ. ①钢结构－文物－世界－
图录 Ⅳ. ①K866.4-64

中国版本图书馆CIP数据核字（2020）第139431号

馆藏撷珍：深圳中国钢结构博物馆馆藏精品图录（第一辑）

深圳中国钢结构博物馆 编

主　　编：周发榜
副 主 编：周爱文　张利锋（执行）
撰 稿 人：张利锋　贺晓光　孙　茜　林晓添

责任编辑：智　朴
责任印制：苏　林
出版发行：文物出版社
地　　址：北京市东直门内北小街2号楼
网　　址：http://www.wenwu.com
邮　　箱：web@wenwu.com
印　　刷：雅昌文化（集团）有限公司
版　　次：2020年8月第1版
印　　次：2020年8月第1次印刷
开　　本：889mm×1194 mm　　1/16
印　　张：16
书　　号：ISBN 978-7-5010-6749-7
定　　价：360.00元

序

  西谚有云：ALL HIS GEESE ARE SWANS，直译过来就是"他所有的鹅都是他的天鹅"，表达的是对自己所有物的珍爱，也就是我们常说的"敝帚自珍"。

  这种视自有物品为珍宝的心理，是人之常情，也是许多行业由来已久的传统——匠人们对于自己生计所系的工具和呕心沥血的作品，总是倍加珍惜。旧时木匠们在使用过自己的斧头之后，都要细细地清理干净并用红布包起来，民间有俗语"师傅斧，恰惜某"，就是把木匠爱惜工具比作爱护自己的亲人。

  以建筑为业的设计师和工程师也是这样一群人。用旧的测量尺、绘图笔，画过的设计稿、结构图，翻阅的参考书、规范集，亲手制作的钢节点，亲身参与的大项目……因为凝聚着个体的智慧，承载着群体的汗水，镌刻着时代的印迹，或成为设计师、建筑师手边的宝贝，或成为一代人心头沉甸甸的记忆。这种记忆，可以激励自己，并同时影响他人，更是属于整个行业的共同财富。

  公元 1631 年，第六次在会试中落榜的宋应星已经四十五岁，他从此彻底断绝了科举入仕的念头，开始潜心收集整理农业和手工业技术知识，最终利用三年时间完成《天工开物》。这本被誉为"中国技术百科全书"的科学巨著，译有多种文本，对各国生产技术发展产生了深远影响，彰显了积累和传承对行业乃至社会发展的巨大力量。

  由中建科工集团举办的钢结构博物馆就是收藏和保护钢结构行业发展见证物的宝库。中建科工集团的员工东奔西走，累计为钢结构博物馆征得各类藏品逾 1000 件（套），其中不乏珍品和孤品；征集过程中，持宝机构和人士割爱见遗，使钢结构博物馆琳琅满目。

  "遗簪见取终安用，敝帚虽微亦自珍"（宋·陆游《秋思》）。我们每一个钢结构人，都应该为自己的职业自豪，为脚下的道路喝彩，也可以通过自己的积累，为整个行业的发展尽一份力。从这一点上说，钢结构博物馆的建设很有必要，钢结构博物馆的收藏极具价值。

  言为心声，欣然序之。

中建科工集团有限公司董事长

深圳中国钢结构博物馆名誉馆长

目录

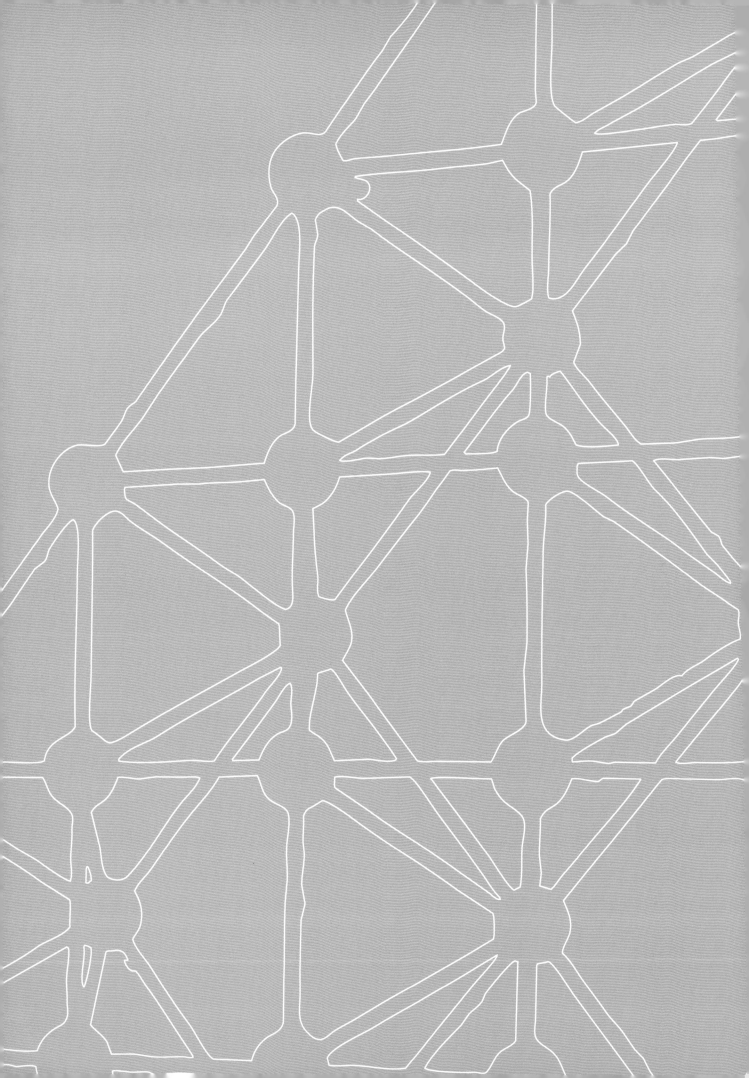

构件、材料
和
模型

四川泸定桥铁索（局部）

古代

铁

单环长：19 厘米

铁环直径：2.6 厘米

重：3.5 千克

"金沙水拍云崖暖，大渡桥横铁索寒。"泸定桥，这座由清康熙帝御批建造的悬索桥，因中国工农红军长征途中的飞夺壮举和毛泽东主席脍炙人口的壮美诗句，闻名大江南北。

泸定桥所在的地区，是四川通往西康、西藏地区的交通要道。为加强与康藏地区的联系，清康熙四十四年（1705 年），清政府决定在河谷狭窄、地势低平、水流较缓的泸定城西建造悬索桥梁，次年竣工。整座桥由 13 条铁索组成，其中 9 条为底索，索间距离 33 厘米，上铺横木板，横木板上再铺八道纵木板作为桥面。另外 4 条铁索则作为行人的扶栏。铁索全由手工锻打成型，每根长 127.45 米，重约 2.5 吨，由 800~900 个扁环扣链而成。桥建成后，为保证安全，每天仅允许定时通行并限制同时过桥的人数。

本馆收藏的这两环铁索身形朴实，色彩斑斓，沉淀着历史的印记，是 2005 年泸定桥大修时更换下来的组件。铁索铸造工艺高超，完全看不出打磨连接的痕迹；泸定桥跨度超过百米，在当时处于世界领先水平，直到 119 年后才被英国的梅奈大桥超越。

本藏品由泸定县文物管理局捐赠。

埃菲尔铁塔铆钉

近代
钢
通长：8 厘米
钉头直径：4.2 厘米
重：340 克

　　埃菲尔铁塔是标志性钢结构建筑，位于巴黎战神广场，由法国著名建筑师、结构工程师古斯塔夫·埃菲尔（Gustave Eiffel）为 1889 年巴黎世博会设计建造。铁塔总高 324 米，共使用钢材 7300 吨，金属部件 12000 个，铆钉 250 万颗。

　　铆钉是钉形物件，一端有帽。在铆接时，利用自身变形或过盈，连接被铆接的零件、构件。

　　这枚铆钉于 1887~1889 年埃菲尔铁塔修建时安装在塔身上，后期养护时更换下来，由法国国有埃菲尔铁塔开发公司捐赠。

启新水泥厂厂房用竹节钢筋 (4种)

近代

钢

长：40 厘米

截面边长：1~2 厘米

重：0.5~1.1 千克

竹节钢筋属于带肋钢筋的一种，用于钢筋混凝土中，这种表面竹节状突起的设计是为了增强钢筋与水泥的结合力。

启新水泥厂位于河北省唐山市中心城区，始建于清光绪十五年（1889 年），由中国近代历史上著名的洋行买办、清末洋务运动的积极参加者、开平矿务局总办唐廷枢开办。中国第一桶（旧时水泥按桶计量）水泥在这里诞生，启新产品"马牌"水泥曾多次荣膺国际大奖，该厂一度成为中国最大的水泥企业，并自建厂以来横跨 3 个世纪连续生产 120 多年，直到 2009 年 8 号窑停产。

本馆收藏的是启新水泥厂厂房使用的竹节钢筋，由中国水泥工业博物馆捐赠。

上海外白渡桥铆钉（2 种）

近代
钢

　　上海外白渡桥始建于 1907 年，1908 年 1 月 20 日落成通车，是中国第一座全钢结构铆接桥梁，也是目前仅存的不等高桁架结构桥。该桥由当时上海公共租界工部局主持修造，由英国豪沃思·厄斯金公司设计并承建，英国达林顿市克利夫兰桥梁建筑公司制造钢构件。百余年来，外白渡桥始终是上海的标志之一。

　　外白渡桥构件由 16 万枚左右的铆钉连接。时至今天，铆接除在小规模铁路桥建设中使用外，已基本绝迹。2008 年 4 月 6 日建成一百年之际，外白渡桥（除桥墩）从原处整体拆除，通过船舶运送至上海船厂进行大修。为了"修旧如旧"，上海船厂特地找到 60 部铆钉机，并空运到沪。最终，这次大修共替换了将近 63000 枚钢铆钉，约占总数的 40%。

　　本馆收藏的两枚铆钉就是外白渡桥大修时更换下来的，由上海船厂船舶有限公司捐赠。

通长：3.5 厘米

钉头直径：3 厘米

重：80 克

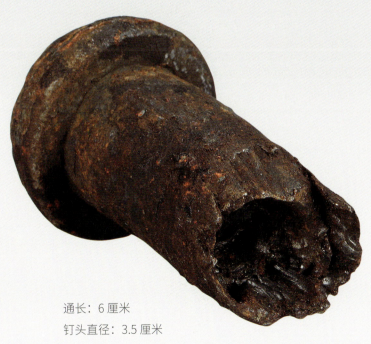

通长：6 厘米

钉头直径：3.5 厘米

重：220 克

金门大桥钢缆（局部）

现当代
钢
长：11 厘米
直径约 7.5 厘米
重：2.2 千克

本藏品是美国金门大桥钢缆的一段余料。

金门大桥建成于 1937 年，是世界上最著名的钢桁梁悬索桥之一，因其新颖的结构和超凡的外观著称于世。大桥南北两侧的巨型钢塔高 342 米，塔的顶端用两根直径各为 92.7 厘米的大桥主钢缆相连，钢缆和桥身之间用 250 对垂直吊索连接。钢缆中点下垂，几乎接近桥身，钢缆两端伸延到岸上锚定于岩石中。整个桥面的重量经由悬索分担到两个桥塔，中间没有任何支撑。

金门大桥的每条主缆由 27572 条钢丝绞成，两条悬索所用钢缆的总长度达到 13 万公里。之所以使用"聚麻成绳"的方法，是因为单独制造一条长且粗的钢缆几乎是不可能的。更重要的是，如果采用单一的一条线缆，一旦发生事故就意味着灾难性的后果，千万条钢丝让维修和事故救援都变得更容易。

如今，金门大桥历经了近一个世纪的风风雨雨，两条主钢缆仍牢固地守护着大桥的安全。

本藏品由李任戈先生捐赠。

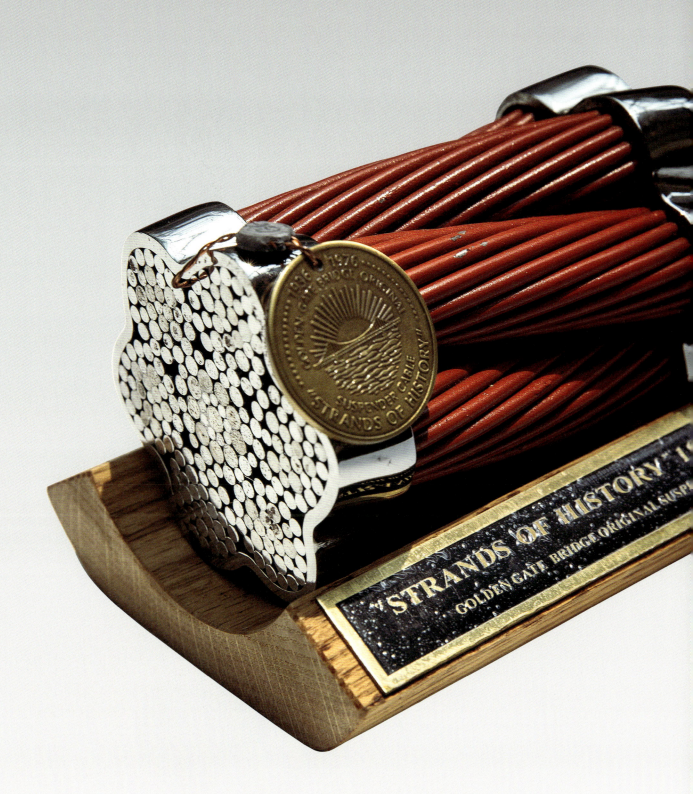

金门大桥铆钉

现当代
钢
通长：10 厘米
钉头直径：4 厘米
重：370 克

　　这枚铆钉曾"服役"于美国金门大桥，在维修时更换下来。尽管历经近百年风雨，钉杆早已是锈迹斑斑，但其顶部却依稀可辨那标志性的国际橘色。

　　建设金门大桥总共使用了大约 120 万枚铆钉，工程量可谓巨大，大桥的设计者和他的队友运用当时最先进的建桥技术，用了足足 4 年的时间完成大桥施工。关于金门大桥铆钉还有一个有趣的故事：1937 年大桥竣工仪式当天，建筑师们突发奇想，希望用一枚纯金铆钉来结束这项浩大工程。不幸的是，金铆钉质地太软，还没铆进去就折断掉进了水里。于是曾经为大桥钻入第一颗铆钉的工人爱德华 · 史丹利，又不得不拿起钻头将这颗金铆钉旋出。竣工庆典因为这样的小插曲而为世人津津乐道。

　　本藏品由李任戈先生捐赠。

焊接球节点模型

现当代

钢

通长：30 厘米

通宽：28 厘米

通高：25 厘米

重：2.8 千克

　　焊接球节点是首先将两个半球焊接成空心球，再将钢管与空心球直接焊接而成的节点，具有构造简单、受力明确、连接方便等优点。焊接球节点适应性强，各种类型的网架，不论跨度和作用荷载大小，当网架件采用圆钢管时，其节点均可以采用焊接空心球节点。

　　焊接球节点 1964~1966 年间由天津大学教授刘锡良成功研制开发，第一个应用工程为天津科学馆。本模型即为刘锡良先生捐赠。

焊接球节点网架结构模型

现当代

钢

通长：33 厘米

通宽：21.5 厘米

通高：5 厘米

重：800 克

　　这个模型是通过焊接球节点组合而成的网架结构。这种结构具有跨距大、强度大、重量轻、造型美观、无须支撑等特点，广泛应用于各种体育馆、大宾馆、大饭店及娱乐场馆。

　　本模型由焊接球节点研发者刘锡良先生捐赠。

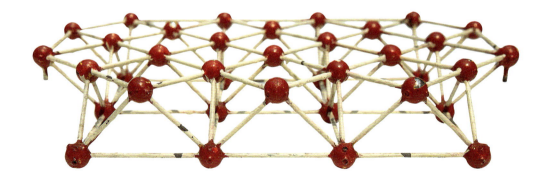

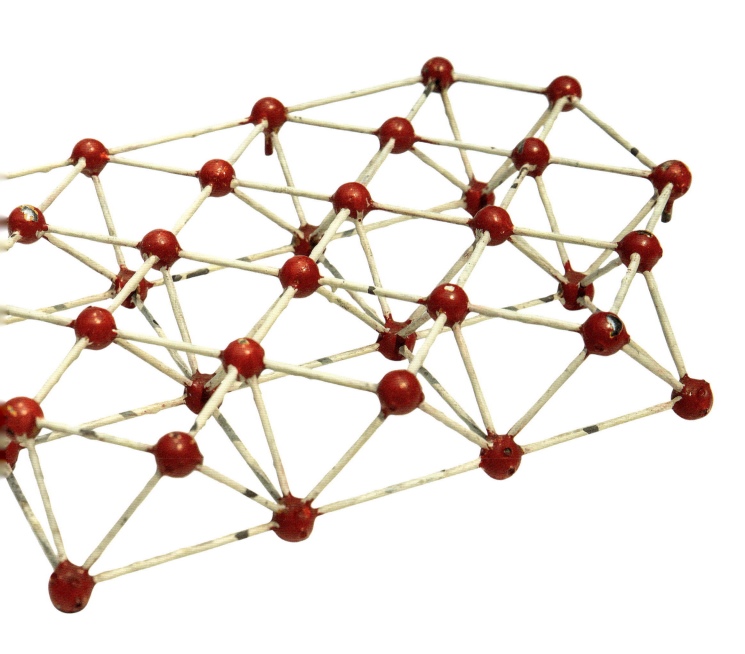

美国纽约世界贸易中心钢构件

现当代

钢

通长：2.48 米

通宽：1.72 米

通高：0.83 米

重：约 3 吨

　　这件巨大的钢构件，是美国纽约世界贸易中心大厦北塔在 2001 年"9·11"恐怖袭击中倒塌后遗留下来的残骸，原属世贸中心北塔顶部天线八边形部分，是本馆的重点藏品之一。

　　世贸中心北塔和南塔在 20 世纪 70 年代初相继建成，其中北塔于 1978 年加装了 110 米的天线。通过天线以及设置在 110 层的电台和电视发送装置，世贸中心北塔对外发送几乎所有纽约市的电视台信号以及四个电台的信号。

　　"9·11"恐怖袭击发生以后，从世贸原址运出的残骸共有 160 余万吨，其中至少有 40 万吨是废钢材。这些钢材大部分通过拍卖售出，用于炼钢，同时也允许民众为了"历史、纪念或教育目的"申请持有。经书面申请，世贸中心所有人纽约与新泽西港务局将上述藏品无偿捐赠本馆。

宝钢 Q500qNHE 耐候钢样品

现当代
钢
长：34 厘米
宽：34 厘米
厚：2 厘米
重：30 千克

　　耐候钢即耐大气腐蚀钢，是介于普通钢和不锈钢之间的低合金钢系列，由普碳钢添加少量铜、镍等耐腐蚀元素而成，耐候性能为普碳钢的 2~8 倍。耐候钢主要用于铁道、车辆、桥梁、塔架、光伏、高速工程等长期暴露在大气中使用的钢结构。

　　中国国家标准将耐候钢分为高耐候钢和焊接耐候钢。高耐候钢的生产原理和焊接耐候钢类似，但是耐候性能更胜一筹。本藏品为高耐候钢样品，由宝山钢铁股份有限公司出品，其牌号中，Q 为屈服强度的"屈"字拼音首字母，500 为最小屈服强度数值，q 为"桥"字拼音首字母，NH 为"耐候"拼音首字母，E 为质量等级。

　　本藏品由宝山钢铁股份有限公司捐赠。

澳门观光塔塔楼拉杆

现当代

钢

长：72.5 厘米

重：1.2 千克

　　澳门观光塔建成于 2001 年，塔高 338 米，是世界高塔联盟成员，高度位列中国第 6 位、全球第 21 位。

　　澳门观光塔塔楼共六层，呈锥形，由辐射状径向钢梁、环向钢梁和钢柱组成稳定的结构体系，上方是二层悬挑钢梁，上铺格栅板。整个塔楼钢构件包括钢柱、钢梁、钢支撑、钢拉杆等约 1400 件，总重约 1300 吨。

　　此拉杆为塔楼钢拉杆的试制件，由陈文革先生捐赠。

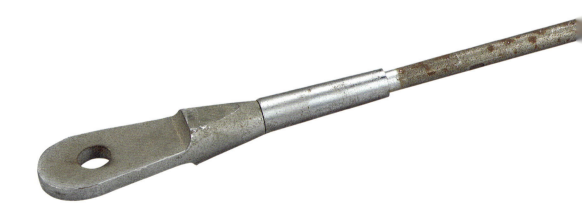

鸟巢 Q460E 纪念钢板

———————————————————

现当代

钢

长：20 厘米

宽：4 厘米

厚：1.1 厘米

重：1 千克

　　这块钢板是河北钢铁集团舞钢公司为 2008 年北京奥运会主体育场"鸟巢"而专项研制生产的 Q460E 钢材，是一种低合金高强度钢。Q 代表钢材强度；460 表示它在受力强度达到 460 兆帕时才会发生塑性变形，460 兆帕相当于4540 标准大气压，而普通钢材的受力强度只有 235 兆帕；E 代表电磁性能为特级的碳素结构钢。

　　在中国国家标准中，Q460 系列钢板的最大厚度为 100 毫米，而建造鸟巢需要钢板厚度达到 110 毫米，在国内外建筑史上，无论钢材生产还是钢结构焊接施工都无可供借鉴的成功经验。随着钢板厚度的增加，由于钢板的压缩比减小，轧制后冷却速度降低，不利于细化晶粒，钢板的强度、韧性很难保证。舞钢经过多次试制，于 2005 年 5 月试制成功上述钢板，确保了国家体育场工程建设顺利进行。Q460E 钢板的技术要求达到当时合金高强度钢之最，创造了国内唯一、世界第一的纪录，实现了"鸟巢"用钢全部"中国造"。

　　2006 年 1 月，使用上述"鸟巢"钢板余料制作的 2008 块纪念钢板发布，本馆收藏的是其中的第 89 块，由周海林先生捐赠。

使用过的牺牲阳极锌块

现当代
锌
通长：42 厘米
通宽：10 厘米
重：2.9 千克

　　牺牲阳极的阴极保护法，又称牺牲阳极保护法，是一种防止金属腐蚀的方法，将还原性较强的金属作为保护极，与被保护金属相连构成原电池，还原性较强的金属将作为负极发生氧化反应而消耗，被保护的金属作为正极就可以避免腐蚀。因这种方法牺牲了阳极（原电池的负极）保护了阴极（原电池的正极），因而叫做牺牲阳极保护法。

　　牺牲阳极消耗快，安设位置及方法必须便于更换，常用材料有镁、镁合金、锌、锌合金、铝合金等。这件藏品即为曾被用作牺牲阳极的金属锌块，它已经因发生了氧化反应而消耗。

　　本藏品由佐敦涂料（张家港）有限公司捐赠。

世界技能大赛（焊接类）金奖作品（3 件）

现当代
钢

　　这三件焊接容器分别是中国选手曾正超、宁显海和赵脯菠在第 43 届（2015 年）、44 届（2017 年）和 45 届（2019 年）世界技能大赛上夺得金牌的作品。它们代表了当今世界焊接件的最高水平。

　　世界技能大赛是最高层级的世界性职业技能赛事，被誉为"技能界的奥林匹克"，其竞技水平代表了各领域职业技能发展的世界水平。自 2010 年 10 月中国正式加入世界技能组织以来，在焊接项目上已先后取得三金一银一优胜的优异成绩并实现三连冠，为祖国争得了荣誉。

　　本馆所收藏的这三件金奖作品由中国工程建设焊接协会捐赠。

第 43 届金奖作品

作者：曾正超

通长：47.5 厘米
通宽：28.7 厘米
通高：39.2 厘米
重：40 千克

第 44 届金奖作品

作者：宁显海

通长：49.1 厘米

通宽：26.2 厘米

通高：38.2 厘米

重：55 千克

第 45 届金奖作品

作者：赵脯菠

通长：45 厘米
通宽：25.5 厘米
通高：41 厘米
重：45 千克

机器人焊接的节点

现当代

钢

通长：65 厘米

通宽：27 厘米

通高：27 厘米

重：20 千克

这是一件由焊接机器人焊接完成的钢结构节点，此类节点通常为钢结构管桁架或网架的组成部分，形状尺寸不一。

工业机器人是一种多用途的、可重复编程的自动控制操作机，具有三个或更多可编程的轴，用于工业自动化领域。为了适应不同的用途，机器人最后一个轴的机械接口，通常是一个连接法兰，可接装不同的末端执行器。焊接机器人就是在工业机器人的末轴法兰装接焊枪等工具，使之能进行焊接作业。

机器人焊接优势明显，一方面能够稳定和提高焊接质量，将焊接质量以数据形式反映出来，另一方面可以提高劳动生产率，改善工人劳动强度，降低对工人操作技术的要求。

本藏品由中建科工集团广东制造基地捐赠。

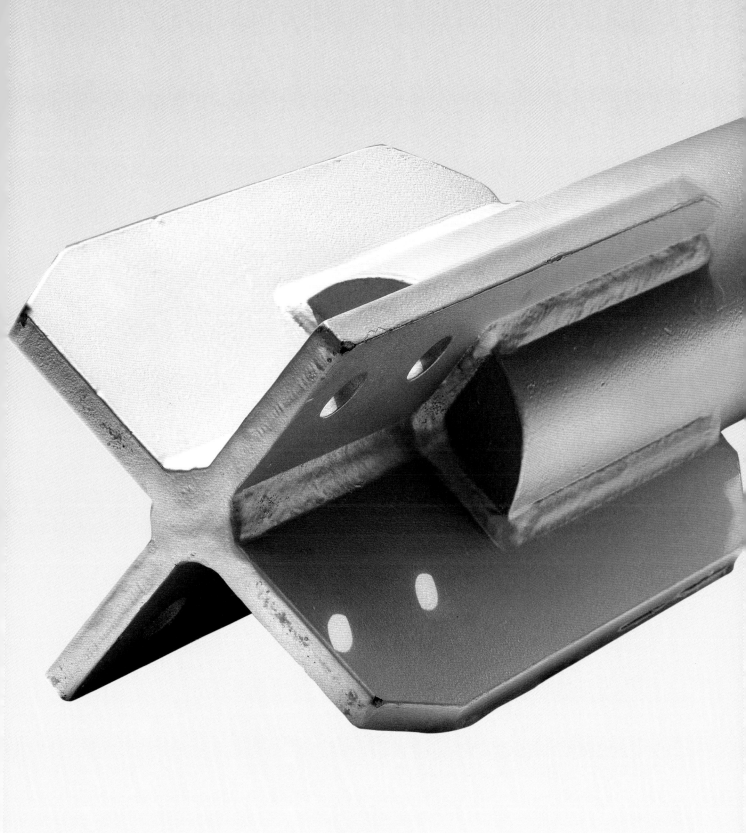

铸钢节点

现当代

钢

通长：52 厘米

通宽：35 厘米

通高：33 厘米

重：98 千克

　　这个多管交接的物体为铸钢节点，即通过铸造工艺完成的钢结构节点。该节点以第 26 届世界大学生运动会主场馆——深圳大运中心最大的铸钢节点为原型，按照 1：10 缩尺铸造而成。

　　铸造工艺是将液体金属浇铸到与零件形状相适应的铸造空腔中，待其冷却凝固，从而获得零件的方法。由于钢管相贯处直接铸造成型，使钢结构受力更加合理，整体结构更加稳定，克服了大量集中焊接造成的应力对整体结构带来的不利影响。

　　铸钢节点可以铸成空间任意形状，使任何形状的建筑造型都可以成为现实。

　　本藏品由江苏永益铸管股份有限公司捐赠。

旋转阻尼器模型

现当代

钢

宽：15.5 厘米

厚：4 厘米

通高：14 厘米

重：600 克

　　旋转阻尼器主要利用了螺旋杆对结构变动幅度的减少和阻尼液对螺旋杆的黏滞功能。阻尼液是一种黏稠状的油，结构震动时，螺旋杆随着螺旋运动，阻尼液充分发挥其摩擦和黏连作用，减缓螺旋杆的运动，从而减慢整体震动的幅度。

　　本模型由日本日建设计捐赠，其原型应用于该公司设计的日本名古屋 MODE 学园螺旋塔楼。

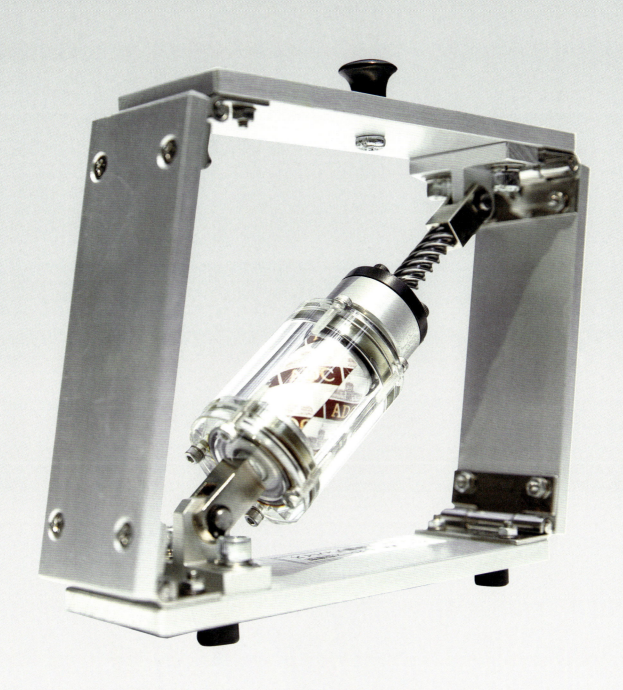

3D 打印节点

现当代

钢

通宽：10 厘米

通高：14 厘米

直径：5.4 厘米

重：500 克

这是一个利用 3D 打印技术制作的钢结构节点。

3D 打印是以数字模型文件为基础，运用粉末状金属或塑料等可黏合材料，通过逐层打印的方式来构造物体的技术。3D 打印技术出现在 20 世纪 90 年代中期，实际上是利用光固化和纸层叠等技术的最新快速成型装置。它与普通打印工作原理基本相同，打印机内装有液体或粉末等"打印材料"，与电脑连接后，通过电脑控制把"打印材料"一层层叠加起来，最终把计算机上的蓝图变成实物。

3D 打印不仅是一种全新的建筑方式，更是一种颠覆传统的建筑模式。它更加高效、坚固耐用、节能环保，不仅解放人力，还能大大降低建造成本。与传统建筑行业相比，3D 打印的建筑不但建材质量可靠，理论上还可节约建筑材料 30%~60%、缩短工期 50%~70%、减少人工 50%~80%。据测算，3D 打印能使建筑成本降低 50% 以上。

本藏品购自奥雅纳荷兰公司。

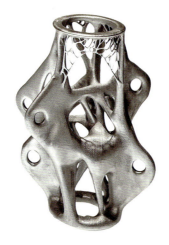

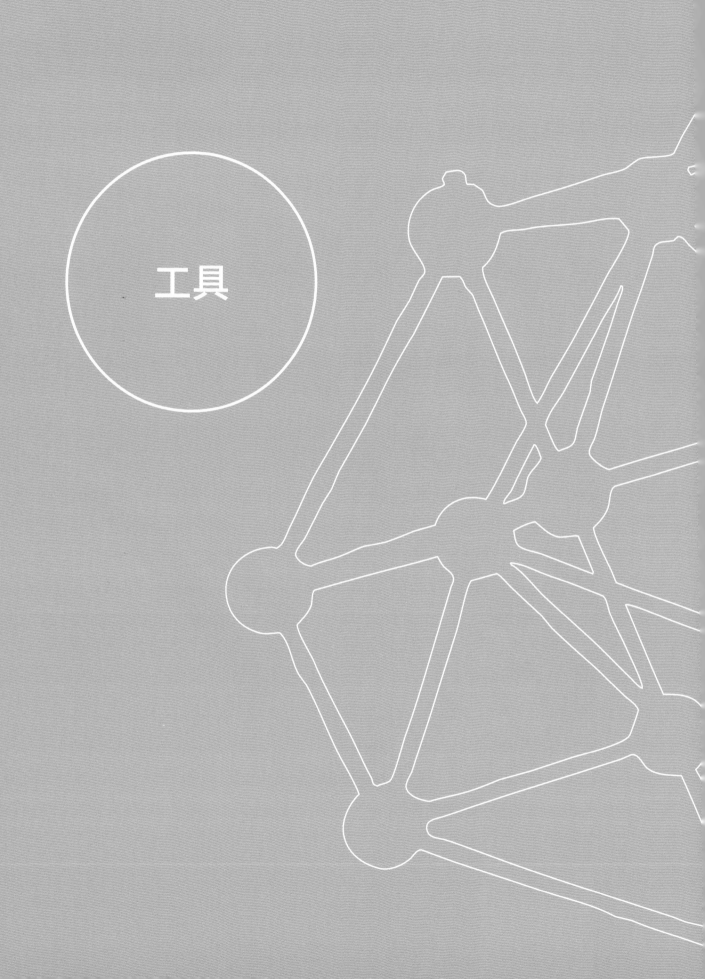

工具

滇越铁路修建者使用的铜钉锤

近代

铜

通长：29 厘米

通宽：15 厘米

重：1.5 千克

　　滇越铁路连接中国昆明和越南海防，是云南历史上第一条铁路，也是中国第一条通向国外的铁路，修建于清朝末年，由法国殖民者建造。滇越铁路全长 855 公里，整个铁路横贯穿梭于滇东南的崇山峻岭之中，地势十分险要，施工条件恶劣。铜钉锤结构简单、材质结实耐用，为滇越铁路施工作业提供了巨大帮助。

　　本馆收藏的这柄钉锤材质为厚料全铜，由云南铁路博物馆捐赠。

滇越铁路人字桥修建者使用的煤石灯

近代

铜

通高：19.5 厘米

底座直径：6 厘米

重：580 克

    煤石灯是指乙炔灯，一般称"嘎斯"灯，"嘎斯"是乙炔的英文音译。"嘎斯"石就是碳化钙（CaC_2），由氧化钙（CaO）与焦炭（C）密闭加强热而成。煤石灯是一个简易乙炔发生器，"嘎斯"石与水反应生成"嘎斯"，就是乙炔气（C_2H_2）。乙炔气点燃与氧反应生成二氧化碳和水，产生亮光，用于照明。

    滇越铁路建设期间，自然条件恶劣，施工设备简陋。作为结构简单、物美价廉的照明工具，煤石灯为夜间和坑洞作业提供了巨大帮助。

    本馆收藏的这盏煤石灯材质为厚料全铜，由云南铁路博物馆捐赠。

线锤

———

近代

铜

通长：7 厘米

最大直径：3.5 厘米

重：200 克

　　本藏品为民国时期使用过的线锤，铜质。线锤需要与线配套使用，统称为锤线。锤线是原始的检验建筑物垂直度的工具，用于校正建筑物是否垂直于水平面，重心是否偏离中心线。

　　本藏品由张开明先生捐赠。

倒链

现当代
合金钢
通长：3 米
重：20 千克

　　倒链又名"手拉葫芦"，是一种使用简易、携带方便的手动起重工具，它运用轮轴原理从而起到省力的作用。倒链适用于小型钢构件的短距离吊装及辅助其他设备配套吊装，常见于钢结构施工现场，起重量从 0.5 吨到 50 吨，起升链条规格包括 3 米、6 米、9 米和 12 米。

　　倒链的外壳材质是优质合金钢，坚固耐磨，安全性能高。使用倒链向上提升重物时，顺时针拽动手拉链条，手链轮转动，下降时逆时针拽动手拉链条，制动座跟刹车片分离，棘轮在棘爪的作用下静止，五齿长轴带动起重链轮反方向运行，从而平稳升降重物。

　　本藏品由中建科工华南大区租赁中心捐赠。

卸扣（2 种）

弓型卸扣	D 型卸扣
现当代	现当代
钢	钢
圆钢直径：2 厘米	圆钢直径：2 厘米
环形内径：6 厘米	环形内径：3 厘米
重：1.6 千克	重：1 千克

　　卸扣是索具的一种，通常作为绳缆末端配件与绳缆配套使用，在钢结构安装、吊运作业中用于绳缆与被吊物之间的连接，仅起到连接作用，便于被吊物的连接与拆卸。

　　卸扣按生产标准一般分为国标、美标、日标三类，其中美标最常用，因其体积小承载重量大而被广泛运用。按型式一般分为弓型卸扣和 D 型卸扣。

　　目前常见的卸扣一般为合金钢材质，改变了过去普通碳钢的历史。选择卸扣时应注意安全系数，一般有 4 倍、6 倍和 8 倍系数，使用时须严格遵守额定载荷，过度频繁使用和超载使用都是不允许的。

　　本藏品由朱光健先生捐赠。

弓型卸扣

D 型卸扣

钱塘江大桥监测传感器（3种）

现当代
钢

　　大跨度桥梁在使用过程中，由于车辆荷载、温度作用的影响，加上混凝土的收缩徐变，会发生损伤。在桥梁结构内部安装检测系统，可以实时地监控桥梁承载能力的变化，及时发现问题，为桥梁养护管理提供帮助。

　　2012年底钱塘江大桥建立了安全监测系统，全桥布置6个动应变测试断面，分别位于各跨的跨中。这三件藏品就是2016年3月大桥监测系统进行升级时更换下来的传感器，其中圆柱形为891-4A型拾振器，矩块形为动应变传感器。

　　拾振器是测振仪中的配件，每套测振仪包括拾振器六台（四台水平向上、两台铅垂向）和六线放大器一台，具有体积小、重量轻、使用方便、动态范围大及一机多用的特点，且拾振器簧片不易损坏，不用调节零位。使用者根据需要，选取拾振器上微型波动开关及放大器上参数选择开关相应的档位，即可获取被测点的加速度、速度及移位参量。动应变测试采用电阻应变片法，由电阻应变片配合动态应变仪进行动应变数据采集。

　　本藏品由中铁桥隧技术有限公司捐赠。

长: 5 厘米

直径: 4 厘米

线长: 26 厘米

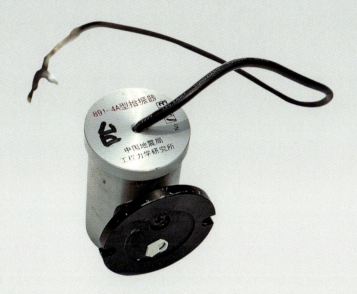

长: 6 厘米

直径: 4 厘米

线长: 30 厘米

通长: 13 厘米

通宽: 4 厘米

通高: 3.5 厘米

线长: 14 厘米

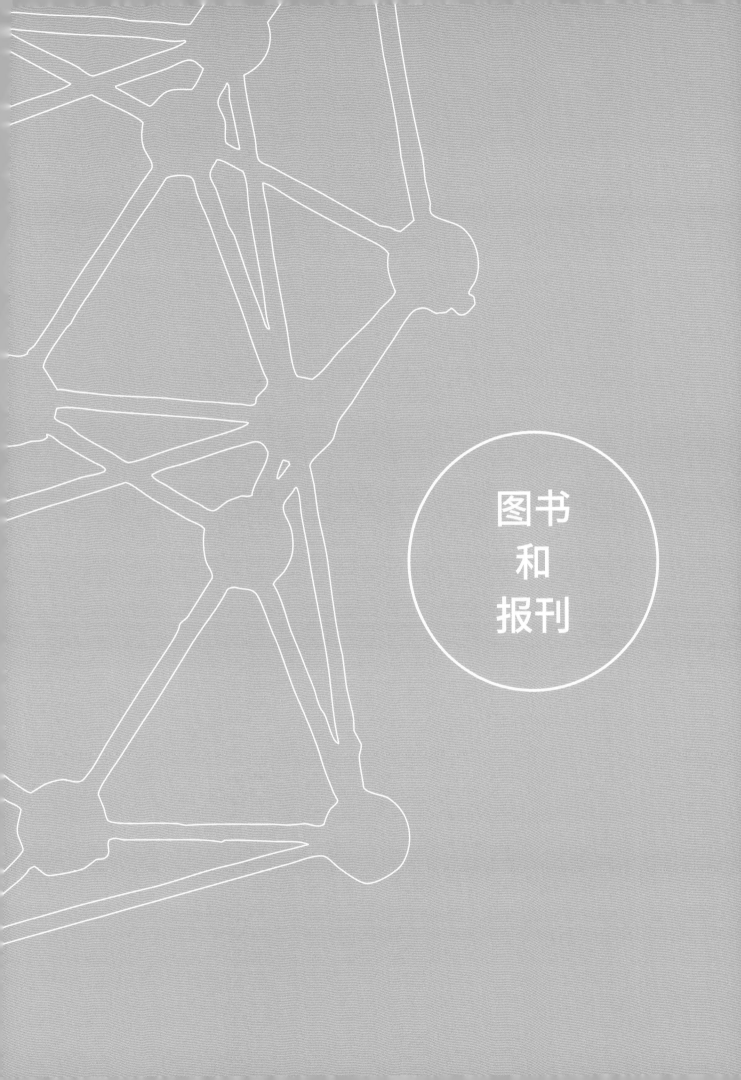

图书和报刊

《国有铁路钢桥规范书》

———————————

近代

纸

16 开

77 页

　　这本《国有铁路钢桥规范书》由中华民国交通部制订，经国务会议议决通过，于民国十一年（1922年）十一月六日由交通部第117号令对外公布。规范语言为中英双语，前半部分为英文，后半部分为中文。正文共155条，内容包括导言、通则、桥面、载重及应力、各部分之支配、设计细则、材料、整料试验、工作法、髹漆等，对国有铁路钢桥从材料、设计到施工工法等均进行了详细规定；附则共5篇，内容包括净空示意图、活重示意图、铆钉之符号、工程师应开示之条款和桥梁招标办法。

　　中国铁路建设起步较晚，直到清末民初方才迎来建设高潮，从1881年至1921年，中国境内共修建了约1.9万公里的铁路。中华民国建立以后，国民政府于1922年公布了铁路建筑的各项标准及规范书，于1932年公布了铁路法，但是由于连年战争，到1949年，全国新建铁路合计仅7400公里，通车里程也只有2.2万公里。

　　本书由陈振明先生捐赠。

交通部製訂

國有鐵路鋼橋規範書

24

shall be securely held in position; furthermore, they shall be so a...
...ed that the sliding surfaces thereof cannot become clogged by...

Bridges on an inclined grade without pin shoes shall h...
sole plates bevelled so that the masonry and expansion surface...
be level.

Fixed Bearings.

87. Fixed bearings shall be firmly anchored to the mas...

Pier-Members.

88. Spans of 30 meters (100 feet) and over shall prefe...
upon hinged or disc bearings, which shall be constructed...
distribute the load evenly over the entire bearing. Bed-plate...
castings, or they may be of rolled steel.

Anchor-Bolts.

89. Anchor-bolts shall not be less than 30 mm. (see o...
quarter (1¼ inches) in diameter.

Anchorage.

90. Anchor-bolts for viaduct-towers and similar...
shall be long enough to engage a mass of masonry weighing...
than one and one-half (1½) times the amount of the net upli...

Camber.

91. Trusses shall be cambered, either by increasing...
of the top chords 1 mm. per meter (⅛ inch per 10 feet); or...
difying the length of member that the floor-line will be stra...
the bridge is fully loaded, and the length of diagonal membe...
calculated accordingly.

The amount of camber of the unloaded bridge when er...
shown on the working drawings, and also the amount of in...
employed during temporary erection at the manufacturer's...

25

Materials

Steel

92. Steel shall be made by the Open-hearth process.

Properties

93. The chemical and physical properties of steel shall conform
to the following limits:—

Elements considered.	Structural Steel.	Rivet Steel.	Cast Steel.
Phosphorus, max. Basic. do do Acid. Sulphur, do	0.05 per cent 0.06 per cent 0.05 per cent	0.05 per cent 0.04 per cent 0.04 per cent	0.05 per cent 0.08 per cent 0.05 per cent
Ultimate tensile strength, in kgs. per mm.²	38.5 to 45.5 { 55,000 to 65,000 lbs. per sq. in. }	31.5 to 38.5 { 45,000 to 55,000 lbs. per sq. in. }	45.5 (65,000 lbs. per sq. in.) minimum
Yield point, in kgs. per mm.² minimum.	21 (30,000 lbs. per in.²)	17.5 (25,000 lbs. per in.²)	22 (33,000 lbs. per in.²)
Elongation, minimum percentage in 200 mm. (8 in.), Fig. I.	$\dfrac{1054}{\text{Ultimate tensile strength}}$ $\dfrac{1,500,000}{\text{(Ult. tensile strength in lbs. per in.²)}}$		15
Elongation, min. percentage in 50 mm. (2 in.), Fig. II.	22		
Cold bends without fracture,	180° flat	180° flat	90°, d = 3t

in whibh d = diameter of pin.
t = thickness of specimen.

《钢木结构》（英文）

近代

纸

32 开

695 页

　　这本《钢木结构》是一本关于现代主要工程结构设计建造的英文参考书，作者为美国威斯康星大学结构工程学教授乔治·胡尔和 W.S. 金尼，1923 年出版。全书大 32 开，共 695 页，分为 11 个部分，内容涵盖建筑、屋顶桁架、短跨钢桥、木桥和栈桥、钢结构罐体、烟囱、结构钢细节、钢结构制造、钢结构安装、钢结构估算和材料等，并附有美国铁路工程协会《钢铁桥梁的一般规范》、美国测试材料协会《建筑用结构钢的观测》以及《桥梁结构用钢规范》等。

　　本书由须子鸣先生捐赠。

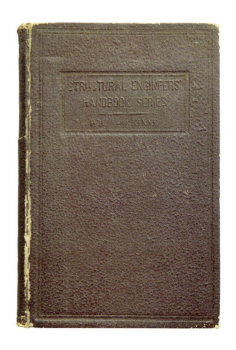

it well to design the connections of girders to columns, and joists to columns, relatively strong, providing continuity across the columns. Details of such connections are discussed in the volume on Structural Members and Connections.

42. Connections to Walls.—All girders and joists entering masonry walls should rest upon steel or iron bearing plates, well painted. An air space should be left around the ends of the joists and girders. In order to allow the girders or joists to fall without pulling the walls over in case of fire, the ends of the timbers are usually cut back, as in Fig. 172. For tying the girders and joists into the walls, iron or steel anchors are used, as illustrated in Fig. 172. These anchors should be approximately ¾ × 1½-in. straps, one end forged into a

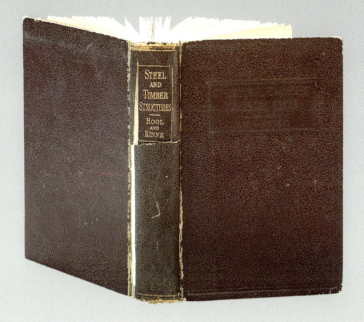

FIG. 172.—Details of connection—timber joists to brick walls.   FIG. 173.—Van Dorn box anchor.   FIG. 174.—"Ideal" wall box.

lug to fit into a notch in the upper side of girder. The portion within the wall may be bonded into the masonry. Sometimes an anchor consisting of a round rod is passed through the wall, and is fitted with an exterior ornamental cast-iron washer on the outside. The other end of the rod may be forged into a flat strap with a lug as before.

Every girder should be anchored into the wall. In the case of joists, at least every sixth joist should be so anchored. Building ordinances usually prescribe in detail the sizes and arrangement of wall anchors.

Joists, closely spaced, entering a masonry wall weaken the walls. Further, unless very careful inspection is maintained, one can never be certain that proper air spaces will be left around the timbers entering the wall. For this reason, there have been developed wall boxes, made of malleable iron, steel, and cast iron, to insure an air space around the joist or girder, and at the same time allow the timber to be self-releasing in case of fire. The tie between timber and wall is secured by a lug on the base of the anchor which engages a notch on the under side of joist or girder. Typical box anchors are shown in Figs. 173 to 175 inclusive. Figure 177 shows a Duplex wall plate.

A third method for support of joists and girders is the wall hanger shown in Figs. 178 and 179. With the wall hanger, no hole is left in the wall. Since the joists and girders with this device extend only to the inner surface of the wall, a saving in timber is made. Since lumber comes in lengths of multiples of 2 ft. only, the use of the wall hanger as compared to the box anchor may mean a saving, in many cases, of 2 ft. in the length of timber—a very considerable item.

42/ Typical Floor Bay Design.—The following example will illustrate the necessary computations for designing the joists and girders of a typical floor bay. The framing plan of the bay is shown in Fig. 180.

FIG. 175.—Lane wrought steel wall box.   FIG. 176.—Duplex wall box.   FIG. 177.—Duplex wall plate.

Data: Office floor; partitions 2 × 4 in., plastered both sides, 12 ft. high; flooring double, under floor rough 1 × 6 in., upper floor 1 × 4 in., T & G; plastered; joists 16 in. on centers; live load for joists, 60 lb. per sq. ft.; live load for girders, 48 lb. per sq. ft.; live load for stairs, 75 lb. per sq. ft.

FIG. 178.—Duplex wall hanger.   FIG. 179.—"Falls" joist hanger.

For approximate dead load, call flooring 2 in. thick at 3 lb. per board foot; assume joists 2 × 16 in.—16 in. on centers; allow 1 lb. per sq. ft. for bridging; assume plaster ceiling weight 5 lb. per sq. ft.; assume girder weight as 2 lb. per sq. ft.

Timber: Douglas fir, dense structural grade, all timbers to be taken as S1S1E,[‡] working stress 1,800 lb. per sq. in. in flexure and 175 lb. in horizontal shear.

Loadings:

Loadings:	Joists	Girders
Flooring	6	6
Joists	6	6
Bridging	1	1
Ceiling	5	5
Girder	0	2
Total dead load	18	20
Live load	60	48
Total dead and live load	78 lb. per sq. ft.	68 lb. per sq. ft.

‡ Surfaced one side and one edge.

《钱塘江桥开工纪念刊》

近代

纸

16 开

115 页

　　钱塘江大桥于民国二十三年（1934 年）11 月 11 日开工，由茅以升担任处长的钱塘江桥工程处编辑开工纪念刊一本，以纪念这一重要时刻，"庶关心人士，得明其内容，便于督责；而在本处同人，则不啻座右之铭，策励所资……"

　　纪念刊中记录了大量与钱塘江桥有关的人物和事件，包括开工典礼安排、交通部和浙江省政府重要嘉宾讲话、承办厂家一览及其代表来宾发言、媒体报道、工程说明和技术资料、人物照片和工程图纸等，是了解和研究钱塘江桥建设计划的重要资料。

　　本书由刘清泉先生捐赠。

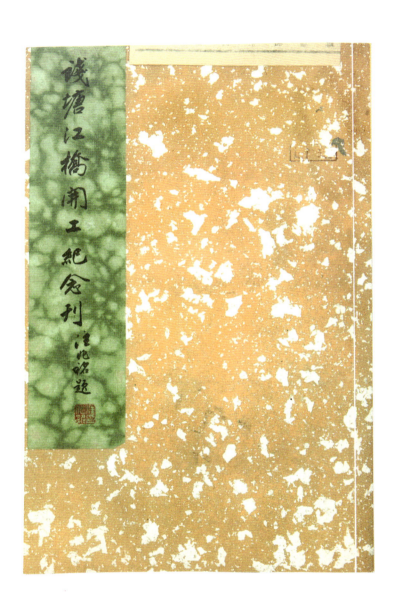

錢塘江橋開工紀念刊　汪兆銘略題

《钢建筑学》

近代
纸
32 开
471 页

美国技术学会出版的土木工程丛书，是美国函授学校教材，丛书注重实用，避免高深的理论。当中引用数学之处，仅到三角法为止，使读者极易了解；书中举例清晰明显，但凡遇到应用计算均附以若干习题，以备学生练习；全套书附图 1600 余幅，极适宜作为教本或自修课本。该丛书在美国学术界久居重要地位，其执笔者不下十余人，或是富有经验之领袖工程师，或为著名大学之专科教授，均为工程学界知名之士。

中国科学社工程丛书以上述土木工程丛书之最新版本（1938 年版）为蓝本，由国内工程界富有学识经验之人士，以简洁明显的文字从事译述。丛书总计约 120 万字，分为 12 册。

这本《钢建筑学》是丛书第 10 册，原作者亨利·J·布特，1940 年由许止禅译述。全书分为 5 篇 34 章，对钢结构进行了全面的介绍，为当时的建筑设计提供了重要的参考文献。

本书由陈振明先生捐赠。

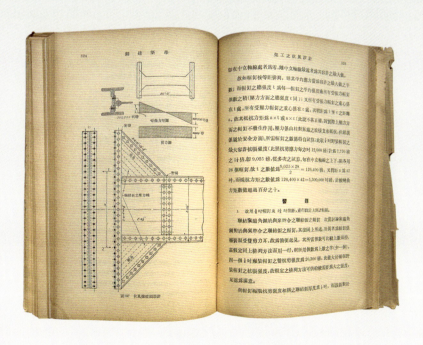

《钢铁屋架设计》

近代

纸

32 开

194 页

这本《钢铁屋架设计》是一本中华民国时期职业学校教科书，编著者周颂文，民国二十九年（1940 年）由商务印书馆出版发行。本书 32 开，共 194 页，分为 4 章，包括总说、屋架之形式、屋架之担负和屋架之设计，并附有中西译名对照表、大料对本有担负及风压担负之应力表等 16 个附表。

当时，商务印书馆作为编印中小学各级教科书的佼佼者，按照国民政府教育部的委托，组织职业教科书委员会，征集全国各省市职业学校自编讲义，择优刊印，供各职业学校选用。本书借鉴国外相关资料，对钢铁屋架的设计做了相对完整的说明，经上述委员会审查通过后公开出版发行。

本书由张开明先生捐赠。

應力，如第六表中之第六行。

最大應力　各桿擔負之應力既已全部求出，即當將其按照前述之四種情形相併合，以求結合之應力，如第六表中之

本書桿員之應力圖

圖十九

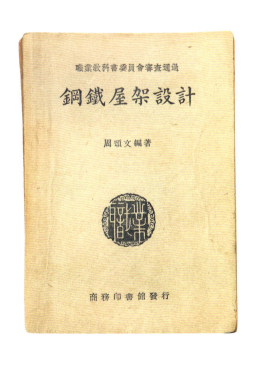

《结构理论》（英文）

近代

纸

32 开

368 页

　　这是一本关于桁架、刚架和空间框架相关结构理论的英文教科书，出版于 1942 年，作者为美国理海大学土木工程学教授海尔·萨瑟兰德和德雷塞尔大学土木工程学教授哈莱·鲍曼。全书 32 开，共 368 页，分为 12 章，包括反应和应力、图形静力学、屋顶桁架、桁架和梁桥、大跨度桥梁、横向支撑和门户、斜坡和偏转、刚架、高层建筑框架中的风应力、不确定的桁架、二次应力、空间框架等内容。

　　本书由刘锡良先生捐赠。

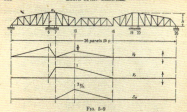

Fig. 5-9

5-5) are indeterminate. The latter would be identical in arrangement with the Beaver bridge (Fig. 5-7) were it not that a horizontal force acting on the suspended span develops horizontal reactions on both main piers.

The computation of reactions is illustrated in the following example.

Example 5-2. Draw influence lines for the vertical reactions at 6 and 7 of the bridge in Fig. 5-9.

Solution. Load at panel point 10. The solution is much simplified by first taking the suspended span as a free body. It is obvious that no reactions are developed acting on this free body except when it carries a load and, consequently, only then does it bring load to either suspended span. It follows at once that each shore structure with its anchor and cantilever arms is entirely independent, carrying any load upon it without help from the other: a load on one does not affect the other.

For a load at point 10 there is no stress in the hanger at 16 and the shear in panel 19-20 being zero, V_{19} must be zero. Considering as a free body the right-hand shore structure, application of the conditions of equilibrium makes it plain that the reactions at points 20 and 26 are also zero. Considering the left shore structure, $V_7 = 1 \uparrow$ ($S_{6z} = 0$); to balance the clockwise couple $1 \times 3 p$ there must be developed $V_9 = \frac{1}{4} \downarrow$, $V_6 = \frac{1}{4} \uparrow$. The rest of the influence line may now be drawn very simply with no computations. The same applies to the second influence line, that for V_7.

Example 5-3. Draw influence line for the stress in bar *a* of the structure shown in Fig. 5-9.

Solution. The free body chosen was the cantilever arm supported by the reaction at 7 and the two horizontal bar stresses. In problems of this type remember that the load travels on a floor system and brings loads to the truss only at panel points.

Example 5-4. What are the reactions on the structure shown in Fig. 5-10 due to the load shown?

Solution. The equations available for use are (1) $\Sigma M = 0$, (2) $\Sigma H = 0$, (3) $\Sigma V = 0$, (4) $M_4 = 0$, (5) $S_{5-4} = 0$; there are five unknowns and the structure is statically determinate. Probably the simplest procedure is to make use of these equations one by one and either evaluate any reaction element directly or express it in terms of another unknown so that there results a free body with all the unknowns expressed in terms of one of them.

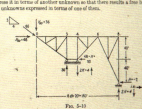

Fig. 5-10

The 60-kip load is resolved into H and V components: since $S_{5-4} = 0$, $V_5 = 36 \uparrow$. Calling the unknown horizontal component at L_0, H, $V_5 = 2 H$ since $M_4 = 0$; also $H_4 = 48 - H$ acting to the left since $\Sigma H = 0$ and $V_4 = 2 H$ down since $S_{5-4} = 0$. This second use of this condition is equivalent to using $\Sigma V = 0$, and there remains only $\Sigma M = 0$ for determining H. The most convenient center of moments is at U_5 since it eliminates three terms of the moment equation, giving

$$-36 \times 60 - 2 H \times 40 + (48 - H)40 = 0$$

whence $H = -2$, that is, acting in direction opposite to that assumed.

5-4. Determinate and Indeterminate Structures. The preceding articles of this chapter give methods for determining whether or not the structures here treated are determinate as regards outer forces. Since, however, these structures are not rigid, as that term is defined in Art. 1-8, they will not be composed of $2 n - 3$ bars, n being the number of joints. Since each joint represents a concurrent coplanar force system in equilibrium, as before, $2 n$ independent equations may be written. For a structure to be statically determinate as regards both outer and inner forces the combined number of reaction components, r, and bar stresses, b, must equal the number of equations. That is, $b + r = 2 n$, or

$$b = 2 n - r$$

and a structure that is both stable and statically determinate as regards *inner* forces will follow this rule.

《武汉大桥计划之历史》（复制品）

近代
纸
纵：30 厘米
横：21 厘米
8 页

　　《武汉大桥计划之历史》是桥梁先驱李文骥先生关于武汉长江大桥建桥计划的文章，成稿于 1948 年初，全文分 7 个部分，包括：北京大学之计划、前铁道部之计划、钱塘江桥工程处之计划、筹建委员会之计划、各次计划评论、扬子江桥另一设计概要和对于计划历史之感想，详细记录了从 20 世纪初开始到新中国成立前，不同机构关于在武汉建设跨江大桥的规划和历史。

　　作者在文首写道："武汉跨江建桥之议始于民国元年……但当时并未详细测量研究，仅系一种议拟而已。具体计划之提出则自民国二年始，其后于民国十八至十九年，二十五至二十六年，三十五年至三十六年，亦续有研究、测量及设计。笔者每次均得参与此项工作，对于各次计划之内容知之颇详……兹特叙述各次桥梁计划之梗概，及经过情形，以备关心交通建设者参考。"

　　在详述建桥计划之后，李文骥针对各计划的优劣进行了分析，并提出建设七孔桥的建议。在文末，他感慨："统观民国成立以来，武汉大桥曾经多次计划，而不得实现，其经过情形，实与国内政潮相表里。政局澄清之际，即有是项计划，应时而生，不旋踵而政局又呈纷乱之象，计划又成泡影。观此项计划之历史，可以占我国政局波澜起伏之迹，如寒暑表之于天气然，有心人于此，当不胜感慨系之矣。"一位爱国工程师的情怀，跃然纸上。

　　本藏品由陶蕾女士捐赠。

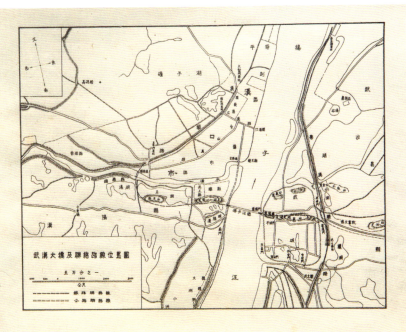

武漢大橋及聯絡路線位置圖

五万分之一
公尺

鐵路聯絡線
公路聯絡線

武漢大橋計劃之歷史　李文驥

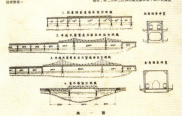

第一圖

北京大學之計劃

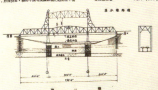

蓋水道橋

第二圖

前鐵道部之計劃

《钱塘江桥》

现当代

纸

32 开

85 页

　　这本《钱塘江桥》，是著名桥梁专家茅以升先生关于其主持建造的钱塘江桥的专著，1950 年由中国科学图书仪器公司出版，是科学画报丛书中的一本。全书 32 开，共 85 页，分为测量与钻探、桥墩、钢梁、第一墩与末孔梁 5 章，并附有钱塘江建桥记、钱塘江桥工程记、工款材料统计表等。

　　本书原稿是茅以升先生在造桥期间陆续写作完成的。当时钱塘江桥的建设引起中外人士的广泛关注，中国科学公司向茅以升约写专稿，逐期发表在《科学画报》上，作为系统报道。作为科学普及材料，茅以升在写作时尽量减少使用术语，也省略了统计数字和计算公式等内容，以便适应大众的理解要求。

　　本书由须子鸣先生捐赠。

錢塘江橋

茅以昇著

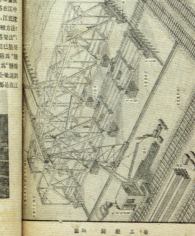

《钢结构设计规范试行草案》

现当代

纸

32 开

82 页

　　新中国成立后，为满足大规模建设工程的需要，当时的国家建筑工程部于 1954 年颁布了《钢结构设计规范试行草案》（规结 -4-54），由建筑工程出版社于 1955 年出版。草案内容包括钢结构设计中的主要原理、主要计算方法、主要材料性能和重要构造要求，共计 59 条，分为 11 章，并附有参考资料 4 个。

　　本草案以苏联 1946 年颁布的《钢结构设计标准及技术条例》为依据编拟而成，仅在建筑工程部系统内试行。1956 年，建筑工程部又翻译出版了苏联 1955 年颁布的《钢结构设计标准及技术规范》，用以代替规结 -4-54，因而本草案终未正式使用。

　　本书由刘锡良先生捐赠。

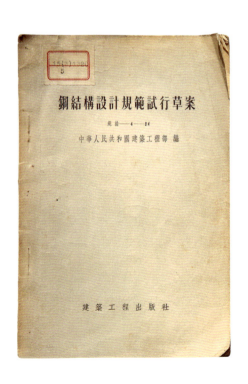

$$\frac{QS_{6p}}{J_{6p}\delta} \leqslant [\tau]$$

式中：φ_b 為按表十一或表十二採用的容許應力折減係數，鉚接工字梁中可採用 $W_{нт} = 0.85 W_{6p}$；

$\qquad S_{6p}$ 為自腰算處至邊緣部分截面全面積對總截面形心軸的靜矩。

軋成工字梁受挽時的容許應力折減係數 φ_b。

軋成工字梁的折減係數 φ_b。　　　　表十一

I(公尺)	2.0	3.0	4.0	5.0	6.0	7.0	8.0	9.0
φ_b	0.98	0.94	0.89	0.82	0.71	0.61	0.54	0.43

鉚成及鉚成工字梁受挽時的容許應力折減係數 φ_b。

鉚成及鉚成工字梁的折減係數 φ_b。　　表十二

$\frac{l}{b}$	\multicolumn{8}{c}{h/δ_m}	
	20	30	40	50	60	70	80	90
	\multicolumn{8}{c}{φ_b}	
10	1.00	1.00	1.00	1.00	1.00	1.00	1.00	1.00
15	0.99	0.97	0.96	0.96	0.95	0.95	0.95	0.95
20	0.94	0.90	0.89	0.88	0.88	0.87	0.87	0.87
25	0.90	0.85	0.77	0.71	0.68	0.66	0.65	0.64
30	0.86	0.68	0.57	0.52	0.50	0.47	0.46	0.45
35	0.79	0.55	0.46	0.41	0.38	0.36	0.35	0.34
40	0.69	0.47	0.38	0.33	0.31	0.29	0.28	0.27

註：(1) 上表中 l 為梁的跨度或受壓翼緣支撐點間的距離；

$\qquad b$ 為受壓翼緣寬度；

$\qquad h$ 為梁的高度；

$\qquad \delta_m$ 為受壓翼緣的厚度（包括翼緣角鋼及蓋板的厚

23

(2) 有蓋板（或型鋼）的受壓翼緣對稱於腹板時，應取蓋板（或型鋼）的寬度為翼緣的寬度 b；

(3) 梁的受壓翼緣不對稱於腹板時，其折減係數 φ_b 應根據受壓緣實度 $\frac{l}{b}$ 算出後，按上表最末一行 $h/\delta_m \geqslant 100$ 內採用；

(4) 僅用翼緣角鋼與腹板鉚成的工字梁，當 $\frac{h}{b} > 3 \frac{\delta_1}{\delta}$ 時，其折減係數 φ_b 應按上表求得的數值乘以 $\eta = 1.1 - 0.01 \frac{l}{b}$ 的值。

式中：

$\qquad \delta$ 為腹板厚度，δ_1 為角鋼厚度。

第 39 條　構件的容許長細比 λ 為其在某平面內的壓屈長度 l_0 與其截面在同平面內旋幅 γ 的比。

受壓構件的長細比不得超過表十三的規定。

受壓構件的容許長細比　　　表十三

結構名稱	構件類別	最大長細比
桁架	弦桿及與支承點結合的各桿	120
	其他構件	150
柱及壓桿	主要的	120
	次要的（牆骨、通風眉的支柱、掾條等）	150
聯結系	所有構件	200

受拉構件的長細比 λ，為其結合點或支撐點間的長度 l 與其截面的最小旋幅 γ 的比。

受拉構件的長細比不得超過表十四的規定。

受拉構件的容許長細比　　　表十四

結構名稱	構件類別	最大長細比	
		直接受動力做	受靜力做
桁架	弦桿及與支承點結合的各桿	250	400
	其他構件	350	400
聯結系	所有構件（拉條除外）	400	400

《钢结构设计标准及技术规范》

现当代
纸
32 开
76 页

　　1956 年，为适应社会主义建设需要，满足结构设计需求，当时的国家建筑工程部技术司主持翻译了苏联《钢结构设计标准及技术规范》。但由于部分条文须结合中国的具体情况，因此并不作为正式设计规范，而仅供各单位参考使用。

　　本规范系由苏联部长会议国家建设委员会批准，1955 年正式颁布执行。规范总计 115 条，分为 9 章：总则、制造钢结构的材料、材料和联结的标准指标、材料和联结的计算指标、基本计算规则、钢结构构件的计算、钢结构联结的计算、钢结构计算的基本指示、构造上的要求，并含钢的特性等 5 个附录。

　　本规范译本由程季达、刘大江译，蔡益燕校，建筑工程部技术司审校，中国工业出版社 1957 年出版。本书由蔡益燕先生捐赠。

苏联部长会议国家建设委员会

鋼結构設計标准及技术规范

（НиТУ 121-55）

中国工业出版社

原本说明

书　名　НОРМЫ И ТЕХНИЧЕСКИЕ УСЛОВИЯ ПРОЕКТИРОВАНИЯ СТАЛЬНЫХ КОНСТРУКЦИЙ（НиТУ 121-55）

批准机关　Государственным Комитетом Совета Министров СССР по Делам Строительства

出版者　Государственное издательство Литературы по Строительству и Архитектуре

出版地点及年份　Москва—1955

鋼結构設計标准及技术规范
（НиТУ 121-55）
程季达　刘大江　譯
蔡　益　素校
建筑工程部校术局审校

中国工业出版社缮写植字排印　中国工业出版社出版
新华书店北京发行所发行·各地新华书店销售

开本787×1092 1/32·印張 8 1/8·字数50,000
1957年5月北京第一版
1962年3月北京第一次印刷·1962年3月北京第一次印刷
印数0001—6,600·定价（精）0.16元

统一书号：15165·1518（建工-208）

---

2. 用在助熔剂下的自动焊接时，采用Св-08、Св-08А、Св-08Г、Св-08ГА和Св-15、Св-15Г号锰钢和高锰钢焊丝，并用相应的助熔剂标号。原采用的焊丝应符合"建筑法规"第一卷第一篇第十章的要求（见附录工表3）。

附注：① 如有充分的根据时，焊接Ст.0、Ст.2、Ст.3和Ст.4号钢所制成的承受静力载荷的结构，可采用符合"建筑法规"第一卷第一篇第十章要求的Э42型的焊線（附錄I表3）。

② 对于焊缝需承受弯曲的冶金工厂的厂房和結构物中吊車梁和桁架以及焊接直接承受振行载荷或震动载荷的结构，应采用：

甲. 当手工焊接時，用Э42А型的焊接；

乙. 当在助熔剂下用自动或半自动焊接时，应采用Св-08ГА號焊絲和AH-348A、ОСЦ-45號的助熔剂或其他實質材料的类型。

第11条(2.6) 铆钉应使用符合"建筑法规"第一卷第一篇第十章要求的Ст.2和Ст.3号铆钉用的平炉热轧炭素钢和НЛ1号的低合金钢制作（见附录工表1）。

第12条(2.7) 螺栓应使用符合"建筑法规"第一卷第一篇第十章要求的Ст.3、Ст.5号普通質量炭素钢或НЛ1和НЛ2号低合金钢制作（见附录工表1）。

縱纹螺栓是使用符合"建筑法规"第一卷第一篇第十章要求的Ст.2和Ст.3号铆钉用的普通質量炭素钢制作（见附录工表1）。

附注：如有充分的根据时，螺栓也可用Ст.0号钢制作。

第三章　材料和联结的标准指标

第13条(3.1) 輥轧钢（厚度4～40公厘）的勻質系数和标准强度，可分别按表1（1）的规定采用。

第14条(3.2) 炭素钢鑄件的勻質系数和标准强度，应按表2（2）的规定采用。

輥轧钢的勻質系数(k)和标准强度R^H　表1(1)

（公斤/平方公分）

项次	标准指标		符号	鋼號 Ст.0	Ст.2 Ст.3 Ст.4	Ст.5	НЛ1	НЛ2
				a	б	в	г	д	е
1	标准强度	抗拉强度、抗剪强度、抗压强度	R^H	1,900	2,200	2,400	2,800	3,000	3,400
2		抗弯强度	$R^H_{ср}$	1,150	1,300	1,450	1,650	1,800	2,100
3		端面承壓强度	$R^H_{см,м}$	2,850	3,300	3,600	4,200	4,500	5,100
4		局部擠壓承壓强度	$R^H_{см,м}$	1,450	1,650	1,800	2,200	2,250	2,550
5		滚軸自由接触的柱向抗壓强度	$R^H_{см,к}$	70	80	90	165	110	125
6	勻質系数		k	0.9	0.9	0.9	0.85	0.85	0.85

炭素钢鑄件的勻質系数 k 和标准强度R^H　表2(2)

（公斤/平方公分）

项次	标准指标		符号	提煉钢鑄件 15Л	35Л
				a	б
1	标准强度	抗拉强度、抗压强度、抗剪强度	$R^H_в$	2,000	2,800
2		抗弯强度	$R^H_{ср}$	1,200	1,700
3		端面承壓强度	$R^H_{см,м}$	4,000	4,200
4		滚軸承壓强度	$R^H_{см,м}$	1,500	2,100
5		滚軸自由接触的柱向抗壓强度	$R^H_{см,к}$	60	80
6	勻質系数		k	0.75	0.75

《钢结构设计手册》（英文）

现当代

纸

16 开

1092 页

　　这本英文版本的《钢结构设计手册》，由英国建筑钢结构协会技术顾问查尔斯 · S · 格雷等人编著，1955 年发行第一版。

　　手册旨在弥补当时普通设计理论教科书与建筑工程实际应用之间的差距，介绍了应用于现代结构的先进设计方法，并以实例作为手册的重要组成部分，相关数据大多以表格形式给出。手册编著得到了当时英国钢铁生产商大会和英国钢铁联合会的大力支持。

　　本书由国家钢结构工程技术研究中心香港分中心捐赠。

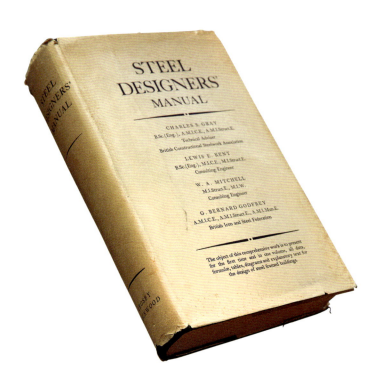

STEEL DESIGNERS' MANUAL

CHARLES S. GRAY
B.Sc.(Eng.), A.M.I.C.E., A.M.I.Struct.E.
Technical Adviser
British Constructional Steelwork Association

LEWIS E. KENT
B.Sc.(Eng.), M.I.C.E., M.I.Struct.E.
Consulting Engineer

W. A. MITCHELL
M.I.Struct.E., M.I.W.
Consulting Engineer

G. BERNARD GODFREY
A.M.I.C.E., A.M.I.Struct.E., A.M.I.Mun.E.
British Iron and Steel Federation

The object of this comprehensive work is to present for the first time and in one volume, all data, formulæ, tables, diagrams and explanatory text for the design of steel framed buildings.

RIGID FRAME FORMULAS
by A. Kleinlogel

Professor Kleinlogel's famous book has been revised and enlarged so that it is now more useful and time saving than ever to the structural engineer. Now available for the first time in English, this handbook of reliable, compact formulas is an invaluable tool for every engineering office.
Illustrated 75/- net

BEAM FORMULAS
by A. Kleinlogel. Translated and revised by Harold G. Lorsch

An indispensable auxiliary to Kleinlogel's well-known *Rigid Frame Formulas*, this volume may also be used independently for the computation of simply supported beams. It contains more than seventy loading conditions covering the entire range of loads that occur in practical engineering. In addition, it presents formulas for general types of loads. An invaluable aid to engineers and designers, it saves hours of computation for statically determinate and indeterminate structures.
Illustrated 40/- net

STRUCTURAL THEORY AND DESIGN
ONE VOLUME EDITION
by J. McHardy Young, B.Sc. M.I.Struct.E. A.M.I.C.E.

'Covers a wide range of theory from the study of materials and the design of simple beams to the deflection of frames, and part of the subject matter is devoted to the design of reinforced concrete. The book is profusely illustrated and each chapter ends with a series of examples selected from Associate Membership Examinations. There are most informative chapters on the analysis and design of building frames, earth pressure, soil mechanics, foundations, etc. The author is to be congratulated on the general layout and the clarity and simplicity of the diagrams and illustrations.' STRUCTURAL ENGINEER. 80/- net

BUILDING AND CIVIL ENGINEERING PLANT
Spence Geddes, E. S. Diplomate, B.T.C. Glasgow

The correct application and efficient operation of plant requires considerable experience gained on works of construction, carrying out those operations on which plant can be employed. The object of this work is to make available a comprehensive book of reference on Building and Civil Engineering Plant so as to make possible a considered approach to its purchase and to ensure its correct application and efficient operation in carrying out the work. It is suitable for the Buyer, the Agent, the Site Engineer, the Plant Manager and all who are interested in plant and its efficient operation.
Illustrated throughout with half-tone photographs, line drawings and diagrams. 80/- net

CROSBY LOCKWOOD AND SON LTD
26 OLD BROMPTON ROAD, LONDON, S.W.7

Grashof's formulæ have been shown by experiment to be approximately correct for values of L/B exceeding 2, but when the plate is square, i.e. $L/B = 1$, the stress is underestimated by 28 per cent. The reasons for the discrepancy in the case of approximately square plates may be demonstrated by reference to Fig. 299. Consider the central strip ab which is the most heavily stressed and will therefore govern the design of the plate. If this narrow strip, which is of unit width, were completely isolated from the re-

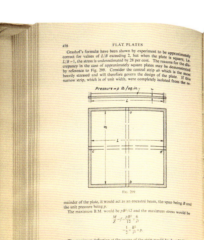

Fig. 299

mainder of the plate, it would act as an encastré beam, the span being B and the unit pressure being p.

The maximum B.M. would be $pB^2/12$ and the maximum stress would be

$$\frac{M}{Z} = f = \frac{pB^2}{12} \cdot \frac{6}{t^2} = \frac{1}{2} \cdot \frac{B^2}{t^2} \cdot p.$$

The maximum deflection at the centre of the strip would be $d = pB^4/384EI$.

Similarly, if a unit strip cd were isolated the maximum stress would be

$$f = \frac{1}{2} \cdot \frac{L^2}{t^2} \cdot p$$

and the maximum deflection would be $pL^4/384EI$.

However, as the plate is homogeneous the strips ab and cd cannot deflect at will. Consequently, some of the load is transferred into the plate adjoining

the strip, the amount of transfer being a function of the deflection of the plate.

Consider the intersection of the strips ab and cd. Let the unit pressure on ab be p_1 and that on cd be p_2. Then $p_1 + p_2 = p$.

If it were assumed that the pressures p_1 and p_2 were constant over ab and cd respectively, then the maximum deflection in ab would be $d_1 = p_1 B^4/384EI$ and in cd would be $d_2 = p_2 L^4/384EI$.

But d_1 must equal d_2.

Hence $p_1 B^4 = p_2 L^4$, but $p = p_1 + p_2$.

Therefore

$$\frac{p_2}{p} = \frac{p_1}{p_1 + p_2} = \frac{L^4}{L^4 + B^4}.$$

Hence, on this assumption, the value $L^4/(L^4 + B^4)$ is the fraction of the load which the strip ab would actually take compared with the load it would take if isolated. This gives rise to Grashof's equation (1).

$$k = \frac{L^4}{L^4 + B^4}$$

GRASHOF'S RULE

Fig. 300

Unfortunately, this assumption is untrue as the pressures are not constant along the central strips ab and cd. At the ends of the strips, as there is no deflection, the pressure must be p; but it gradually diminishes, at varying rates along each strip, until the centre of the plate is reached. The effect of these changes in pressure may be shown by Fig. 300, which is a diagram relating to an approximately square plate. The shaded portion shows the load which Grashof's formula assumes to act throughout the strip ab. The unshaded portion is the amount it ignores.

Obviously rational formulæ must take the unshaded portion into account. A number of investigators have evolved coefficients to modify Grashof's basic formula, but here it is proposed to give those evolved by C. C. Pounder, which agree very closely indeed with experimental data.

1957 年 10 月 16 日《人民日报》

现当代

纸

纵：52 厘米

横：38 厘米

　　1957 年 10 月 15 日，"万里长江第一桥"武汉长江大桥正式通车。次日出版的《人民日报》在头版头条报道了这一消息，题目为"火车飞驰过长江——千年理想成现实，万众欢腾庆通车"。

　　本藏品由夏利莹女士捐赠。

人民日报

1948年6月15日创刊　·　第3386号　地址　北京王府井大街117号

1957年10月
16
星期三
丁酉年
八月二十三
今日天气预报

上图：长江大桥全景

火車飛馳過長

千年理想成現實 萬众歡騰慶

（本报记者 刘长忠 吕相友摄）

表彰苏联专家对长江大桥的创造性贡献

国务院授予西林同志感謝狀

鐵道部授予格列佐夫等九同志感謝狀

从北京开往凭祥的列车，在万人欢呼声中第一次驰过长江大桥
本报记者 刘长忠 吕相友摄（無綫电傳真）

汽车队伍浩浩荡荡通过长江大桥公路桥面
新华社记者 赵敬一摄（無綫电傳真）

《武汉长江大桥》

现当代

纸

长：26 厘米

宽：18.5 厘米

18 页

　　这本书是关于武汉长江大桥建造的图录，由铁道部新建铁路工程总局武汉大桥工程局汇编，1957 年 10 月由长江文艺出版社出版，新华书店武汉发行所发行。全书共 18 页，书中介绍了武汉长江大桥的筹建、工程的全貌、工程数据、新的桥梁基础施工方法、建桥者的劳绩、全国的支援、苏联专家的技术援助等，并配有 21 张照片与图画。

　　本书由陶蕾女士捐赠。

武漢長江大橋

1957.10.

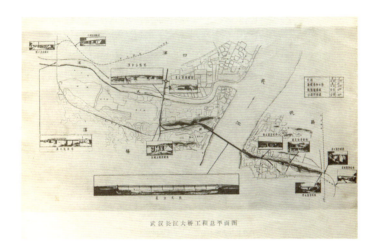

武汉长江大桥工程总平面图

《建设金门大桥——一位施工者的口述历史》（英文）

现当代

纸

32 开

195 页

这本英文版书籍，作者为哈维·施瓦茨，2015 年由美国华盛顿大学出版社出版。本书分为六个章节，分别为：金门大桥概述、采访旧金山建筑工人、采访旧金山钢结构工人、旧金山建筑工人传记、旧金山钢结构工人传记、旧金山传记。

本书由李任戈先生捐赠。

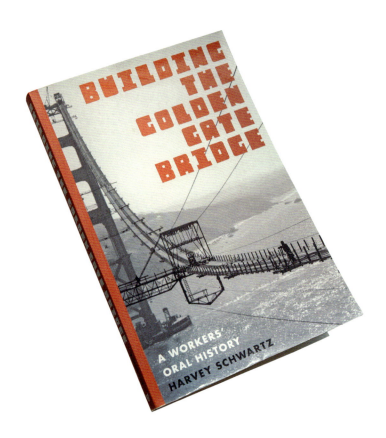

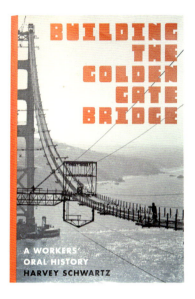

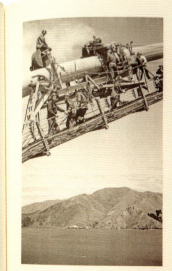

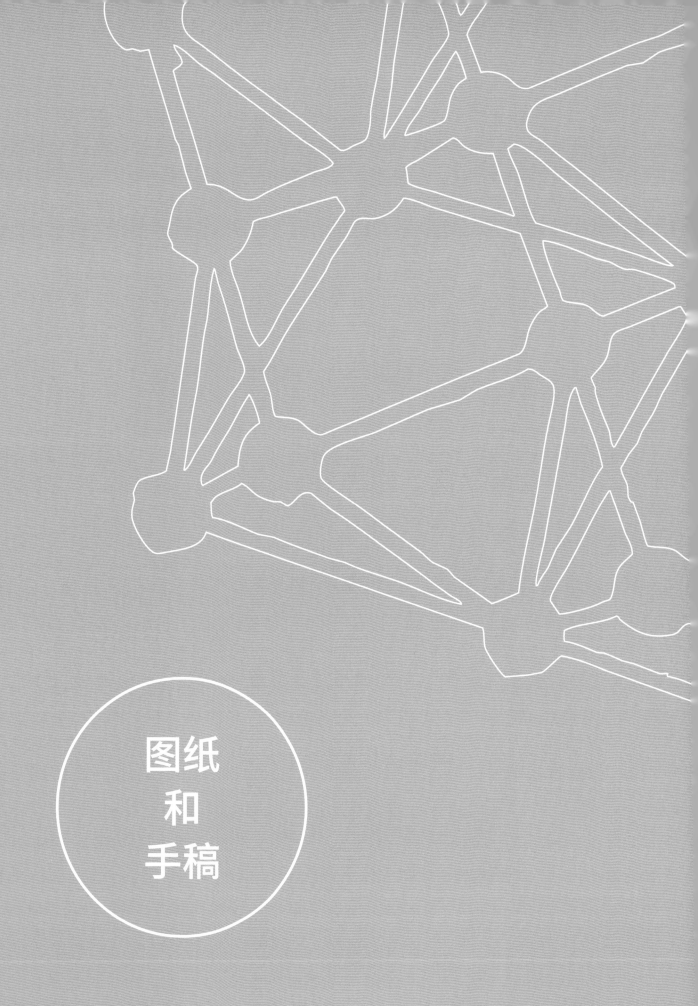

图纸
和
手稿

《武汉大桥计划之历史》推荐函（复制品）

近代

纸

纵：30 厘米

横：21 厘米

　　这是 1949 年 3 月中原临时人民政府出具的《武汉大桥计划之历史》推荐函草稿【工交字第 324 号（本府）呈中央政府铁道部】。

　　推荐函原文如下："接到中南局一月十四日转来李文骥新编之《武汉大桥计划历史》一书，特转呈贵部研究参考。查李文骥在工程界服务三十余年，对桥梁工程研究及经验颇为丰富，兹检送该计划书一份，供作勘探修建武汉大桥之参考（附武汉大桥计划之历史一份）。李文骥通信处：杭州钱塘江桥工程处。"函件具名"主席邓，副主席吴、李"，并加盖"中原临时人民政府印"红色印章。

　　这篇手稿为中原临时人民政府向铁道部推荐李文骥先生所著《武汉大桥计划之历史》的函件，具名"邓、吴、李"应分别指当时中原临时人民政府主席邓子恢和副主席吴芝圃、李一清。本展品见证了李文骥先生所著《武汉大桥计划之历史》的价值，也折射了中原临时人民政府兴建武汉长江大桥的强烈愿望。涂改之处颇多，应为函件草稿，十分珍贵。

　　本藏品复制自湖北省档案馆。

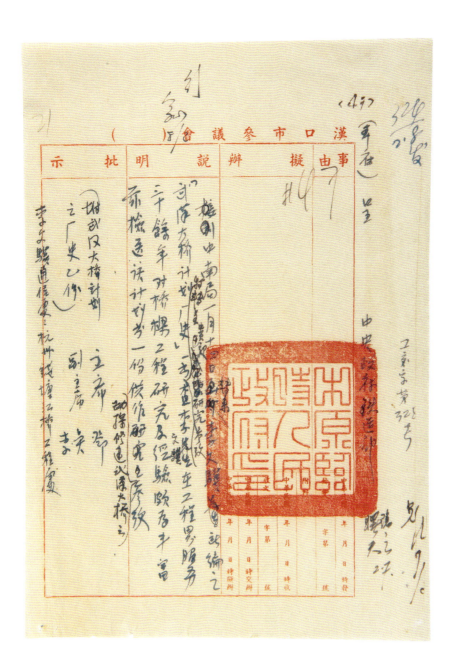

漢口市參議會

事由	擬辦	說明	批示

由呈

年月日時發 字第 號
年月日時收 字第 號
年月日時交辦
年月日時催辦 字第 號

香港中国银行大厦建筑设计图（复制品）

现当代

纸

纵：1 米

横：0.9 米

　　香港中国银行大厦由贝聿铭建筑师事务所设计，1985 年 4 月动工，1989 年建成。大厦地上 70 层，楼高 315 米，加顶上两杆的高度共有 367.4 米，建成时是全亚洲最高的建筑物，也是美国地区以外最高的摩天大楼。大厦外型像竹子的节节高升，象征着力量、生机、茁壮和锐意进取的精神，基座的麻石外墙代表长城，象征中国。

　　楼高加上香港当地台风季节强劲的风力，使得建筑物的结构系统需要非比寻常的解决方式。整座大楼使用的是由八片平面钢支撑和五根型钢混凝土柱所组成的"大型立体支撑体系"混合结构，充分发挥了两种材料的优势。

　　本藏品为复制品，由国家钢结构工程技术研究中心香港分中心捐赠。

NORTHEAST ELEVATION

NORTHWEST ELEVATION

WINDOW WASHING DAVIT CAR ACCESS

WINDOW WASHING INTERMEDIATE ACCESS PANEL

WINDOW WASHING STAGING ACCESS PANELS

OPERABLE SASH, TYPICAL

WINDOW WASHING INTERMEDIATE ACCESS PANEL

WINDOW WASHING INTERMEDIATE ACCESS PANELS

WINDOW WASHING STAGING ACCESS PANELS

WINDOW WASHING INTERMEDIATE ACCESS PANEL

AUTOMATICALLY OPENED SMOKE EXHAUST PANELS

WINDOW WASHING DAVIT CAR ACCESS

WINDOW WASHING DAVIT CAR ACCESS

WINDOW WASHING INTERMEDIATE ACCESS PANEL

WINDOW WASHING STAGING ACCESS PANELS

OPERABLE SASH, TYPICAL

EL 263.333 STOREY 64

EL 213.333 STOREY 51

EL 165.665 STOREY 38

EL 105.333 STOREY 31

EL 80.000
EL 83.333 STOREY 17

EL 13.333 STOREY 3

EL 293.333 STOREY 70

EL 245.333 STOREY 57

EL 189.333 STOREY 44

EL 133.333 STOREY 31

EL 13.333 STOREY 3

NOTE: SHADED AREAS @ TOWER REPRESENT SPANDREL GLASS

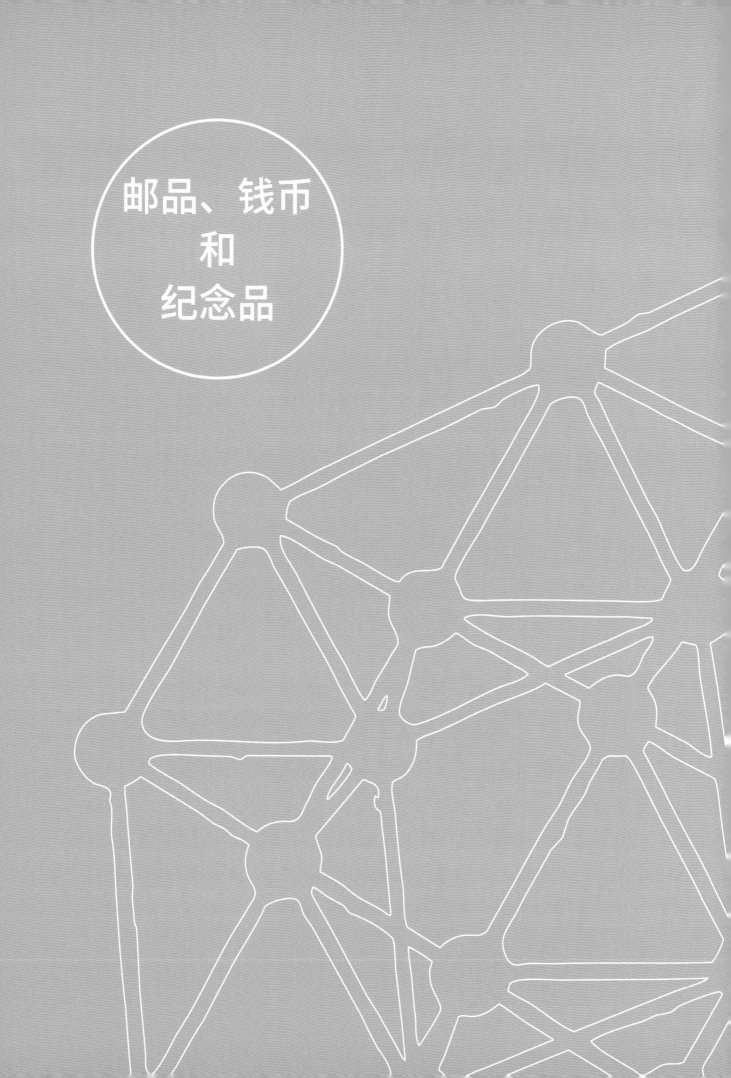

邮品、钱币
和
纪念品

广州市立银行十元纸币

近代
纸
长：16 厘米
宽：10 厘米

　　这枚广州市立银行十元纸币发行于中华民国二十二年（1933 年），正面中间图片为著名的钢结构建筑——中山纪念堂，背面为孙中山先生头像。纸币由伦敦华德路公司印制，编号 C462502，正面为中文，上书"凭票即付持票人通用银毫""订明见票无息支付不报遗失票内字迹原无添改此据"字样，并印有行长陈仲璧、副行长黄湖签名，背面为英文。

　　中山纪念堂于 1929 年 1 月动工，1931 年 11 月完工，由"中国近现代建筑的奠基人"吕彦直设计。其八角形攒尖屋顶由 30 米跨的 4 个桁架成 45°相交构成，堂内不设一柱，是当时国内跨度最大的会堂建筑。

　　本藏品由张开明先生捐赠。

廣州市立銀行

拾圓

持票人通用銀毫
憑票即付

訂明見票無息支付不報遺
失票內字跡原無添改此據

拾圓整

行長
陳仲琦

副行長
黃寶堅

中華民國二十三年印
徐敬華臨鐫公司印

天津金汤桥明信片

近代

纸

长：15 厘米

宽：10 厘米

这是以天津金汤桥为主题的英文明信片，印发时间不详。

金汤桥位于天津海河上，桥长 76.4 米，总宽 10.5 米，是天津市现存最早建造的大型铁桥之一，也是目前国内唯一的钢制平转式开启桥。该桥始建于 1906 年，由津海关道、奥意租界领事署及比商天津电车电灯公司合资建造，命名为"金汤桥"，取"固若金汤"之意。

本藏品由张开明先生捐赠。

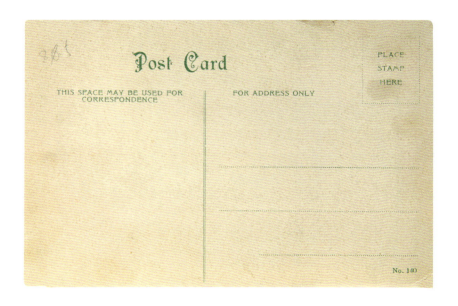

Tientsin, Austrian Bridge
Tientsin, Oesterreichische Brücke

加拿大蒙特利尔世博会纪念封

现当代
纸
长：16 厘米
宽：9 厘米

这枚加拿大蒙特利尔世博会主题纪念信封，发行于 1967 年 5 月 25 日。

蒙特利尔世博会主题为：人类与世界，共有 62 个国家参加了这次盛会。本届世博会是欣欣向荣的加拿大献给世界的礼物，也是世博会一百多年历史中空前成功的一届。1967 年，加拿大举国人口约 2100 万，而蒙特利尔世博会的参观人次超过了 5000 万。这种广泛的民众参与度，无论在当时还是现在，都是难以想象的。

纪念封上巨大的圆球建筑，就是美国艺术家、发明家、科学家巴克敏斯特·富勒设计的美国馆，也称为"富勒球"。美国馆圆球直径 76 米，三角形金属网状结构合理地组合成一个球体。整个设计简洁、新颖，没有任何多余的材料，建筑就像一个精致漂亮的水晶球，白天在日光下闪闪发光，夜晚则通体灯火通明。

本藏品由张利锋先生捐赠。

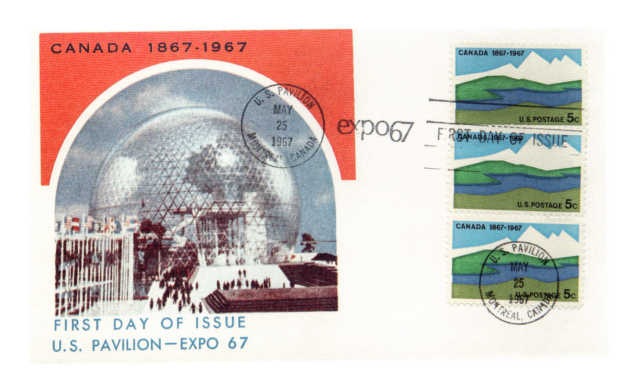

南京长江大桥合龙纪念章

现当代

铝

长：3 厘米

宽：1.2 厘米

重：1.5 克

这枚铝质像章正面为金、红、白三色，印有毛泽东主席头像、大桥图案及"自力更生"4 个字，背面为金色，刻有"南京长江大桥合拢是毛泽东思想的伟大胜利"。

南京长江大桥正式开工于 1960 年 1 月 18 日，整个建设过程充满曲折艰辛。大桥开工后不久，由于中苏关系破裂，苏联拒绝继续供应钢材。1961 年，中国决定使用国产钢材，经艰苦攻关，鞍山钢铁公司成功研制出符合要求的"16 锰"桥梁钢，此后生产该型号钢材 1.4 万吨，保证了大桥钢梁的架设。1966 年 11 月，开始从两岸相向架设正桥钢梁。1967 年 8 月 16 日，正桥钢梁在 4 号墩合龙。

本藏品由张开明先生捐赠。

自力更生

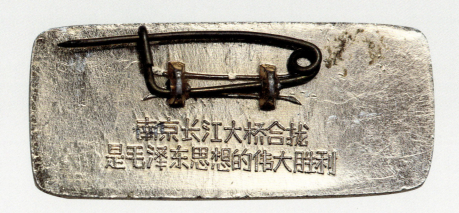

南京长江大桥合拢
是毛泽东思想的伟大胜利

兰州中山桥明信片（2种）

现当代

纸

长：15 厘米

宽：10 厘米

这是以兰州中山桥为主题的明信片，2002 年发行。

兰州中山桥俗称"中山铁桥""黄河铁桥"，1909 年建成通车，是万里黄河上第一座真正意义上的桥梁，素有"天下黄河第一桥"的美誉，1928 年为纪念孙中山先生而改名为"中山桥"。桥长 234 米，宽 7.5 米，共有 4 墩 5 跨，是典型的钢结构桥梁，桥身采用简支铆接钢桁梁结构，上方置弧形钢架拱梁。2006 年，这座百年老桥被国家文物局列为第六批国家重点文物保护单位。

本藏品由张开明先生捐赠。

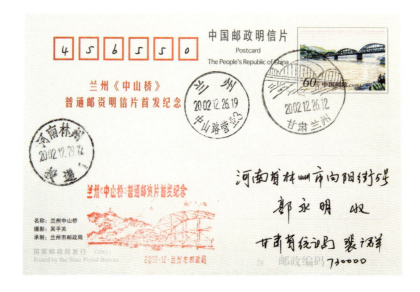

2002(2800)-0096

上海外白渡桥修缮恢复通车——暨亮灯仪式纪念封

现当代

纸

长：22 厘米

宽：12 厘米

2008 年 4 月 6 日，外白渡桥除桥墩以外部分从原处拆下，送往上海船厂进行了历时 10 个月的修缮。2009 年 2 月 26 日，这座百年名桥以原貌回归复位，4 月 10 日举行恢复通车暨亮灯仪式，现场限量发售"百年外白渡桥修缮恢复通车——暨亮灯仪式纪念封"共 20100 个，本纪念封即为其中之一。

本藏品由须子鸣先生捐赠。

天津解放桥明信片

现当代

纸

长：15 厘米

宽：10 厘米

这是以天津解放桥为主题的明信片，具体印发时间不详。

解放桥位于天津火车站（东站）与解放北路之间的海河上，是一座双叶立转式开启式钢结构桥梁，桥长 98 米，桥面宽 19.5 米。解放桥建成于 1927 年，原名"万国桥"，因当时的天津有英、法、俄、美、德、日、意、奥、比等 9 国租界，故得此名。而此桥位于法租界入口处，又是由法租界工部局主持建造的，所以当时天津民众也称它为"法国桥"。抗日战争胜利后，国民政府以蒋介石的名字命名，叫做"中正桥"。1949 年天津解放后此桥正式更名为"解放桥"，并沿用至今。

本藏品由王娟女士捐赠。

天津市邮政广告公司发布　14-120105-11-0006-004

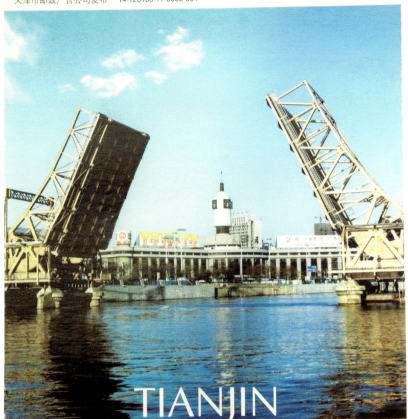

TIANJIN

天津·解放桥

广州海珠桥大修竣工通车纪念封

现当代

纸

长：22.5 厘米

宽：12 厘米

海珠桥是广州市第一座横跨珠江的桥梁，建成于 1933 年，原为三孔下承式简支钢桁架桥，由美国马克敦公司承建。

海珠桥建成后先后进行过几次维修，其中 1995 年维修时采用自锚式吊索方案，桥梁变为三孔式自锚式悬索吊桥，也就是今天所见的模样。2012 年 2 月 28 日起，海珠桥再次大修，耗时 18 个月，于 2013 年 8 月底完工，9 月 1 日恢复通车。维修后海珠桥的桥心高度提高至 8.7 米，承载能力提升至 20 吨，边桥增加了盲道，并设置了景观墙。广州市海珠区集邮协会于 2013 年 8 月印刷发行主题纪念封 2000 枚，以资纪念。

本藏品由广州市国家档案馆捐赠。

163412

广州海珠桥大修竣工通车

2013.8

中国邮政

¥000.70

粤AA352

印 刷 品
IMPRIMES

黑龙江省大庆市银浪村5-2-32信箱

支 玉 杰 老师收

广州芳村大道205号楼特森前下江南邮局   **邮政编码**   510308

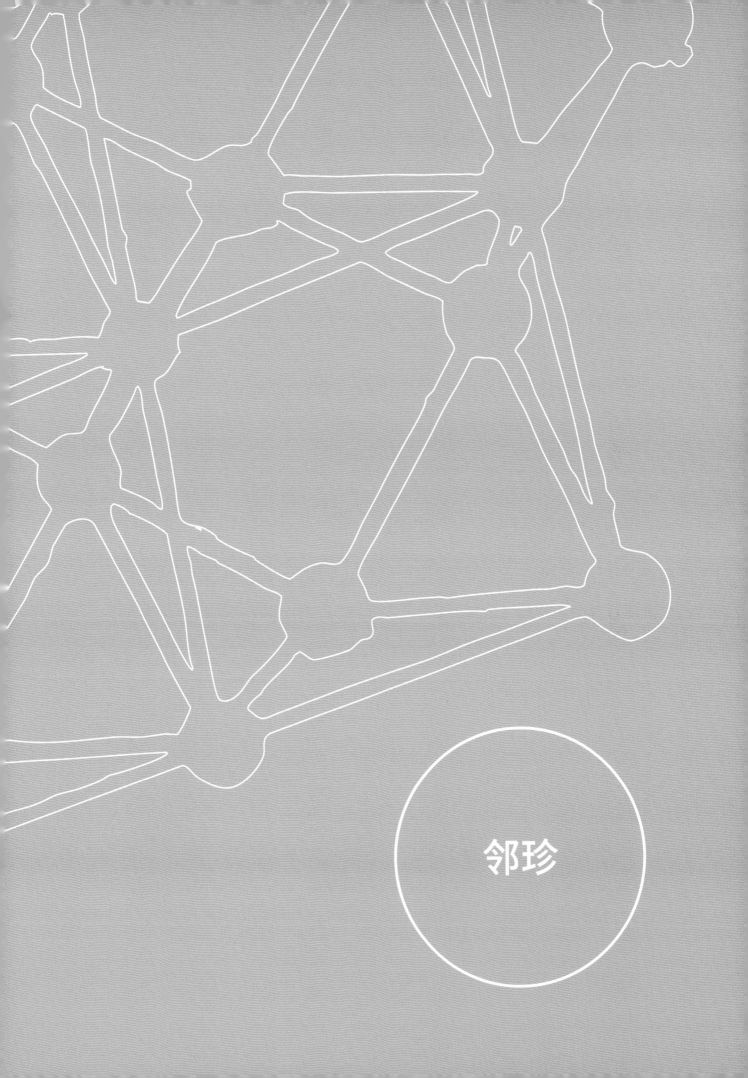

邻珍

京张铁路钢轨（局部）

近代

钢

长：56.5 厘米

通宽：11 厘米

高：13 厘米

重：25 千克

　　京张铁路是第一条由中国人自行设计建造的铁路，由詹天佑担任总工程师，1905 年 9 月开工修建，1909 年正式通车。全线从丰台柳村为起点，经关沟至张家口站，全长 201.2 公里，共建造 14 个车站、4 条隧道和 125 座桥梁，其中钢桥 121 座。

　　这段刻有"K.T.P.E. R.S.W. 1909 V."字样、制造于 1909 年的京张铁路钢轨，由北京铁路局张家口车务段捐赠。

刨刃

———

近代

钢

长：8.5 厘米

宽：5.5 厘米

厚：0.7 厘米

重：200 克

刨刀是用于刨削加工的刀具。刨削加工常见于传统建筑和制造领域，是应用比较广泛且简单的加工平面、凹槽的加工方法。

刨刃是刨刀的主要组成部件。本馆收藏的这枚刨刃，为伪满时期物品，刻有"山林""保证使用"字样。

本藏品由张开明先生捐赠。

小型台钳

近代

钢

通长：7.5 厘米

通宽：2 厘米

通高：10.5 厘米

重：300 克

　　台钳是装在钳工台上、用钳口夹稳加工工件的工具，为钳工必备工具。它也是钳工名称的由来，因为钳工的大部分工作都是在台钳上完成的，比如锯、锉、錾以及零件的装配和拆卸。

　　台钳整体由钳体、底座、导螺母、丝杠、钳口体等组成。活动钳身通过导轨与固定钳身的导轨作滑动配合。丝杠装在活动钳身上，可以旋转，但不能轴向移动，并与安装在固定钳身内的丝杠螺母配合。当摇动手柄使丝杠旋转，就可以带动活动钳身相对于固定钳身作轴向移动，起夹紧或放松的作用。

　　本藏品由张开明先生捐赠。

《昭和制钢所廿年志》（日文）

近代
纸
16 开
422 页

这本《昭和制钢所廿年志》，编辑者为浅轮三郎，发行者为箱崎正吉，印刷者为杉山退助，由株式会社昭和制钢所发行，是不对外发售的内部资料，印刷发行年代为 1940 年。

昭和制钢所是鞍山钢铁厂的前身，由日本侵略者设立，其历史可以追溯至 20世纪初期。1909 年，日本侵略者派人非法勘探了东鞍山等 8 个铁矿区，后来攫取了 8 个矿区的开采权。1918 年成立"鞍山制铁所"。1931 年"九·一八"事变后，日本占领了东北全境。1933 年日本政府在军部的支持下，将原来定在朝鲜的昭和制钢所改迁鞍山，由"满铁"全额出资，在鞍山制铁所已有的基础上兴建制钢厂、轧钢厂，成为钢铁联合企业。随后，昭和制钢所兼并了鞍山制铁所。1943 年，昭和制钢所生产能力达到峰值。

本书语言为日语，共 422 页，约 10 万字，分为总务篇、采矿篇、铣铁篇、制钢篇、化学工业篇、动力篇、工务篇、研究所、商务篇、经理篇、统计、附带设施、年谱等 13 个篇章，并辅以插图 585 幅，内容非常丰富。这本年志不仅是日本钢铁产业发展的记录，也是日本侵华的罪证，弥足珍贵。

本书由刘锦章先生捐赠。

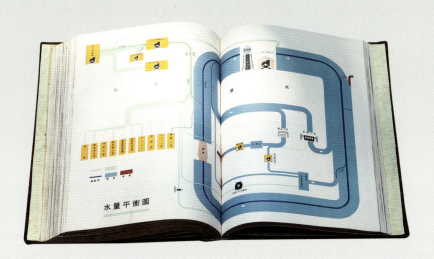

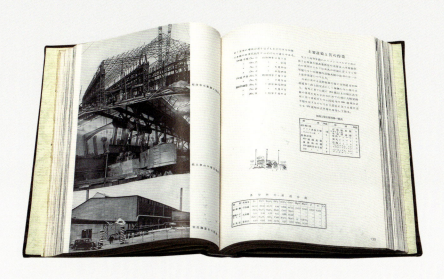

THE SELECTED COLLECTIONS OF STEEL STRUCTURE MUSEUM

VOLUME I

Compiled by Steel Structure Museum

Cultural Relics Press

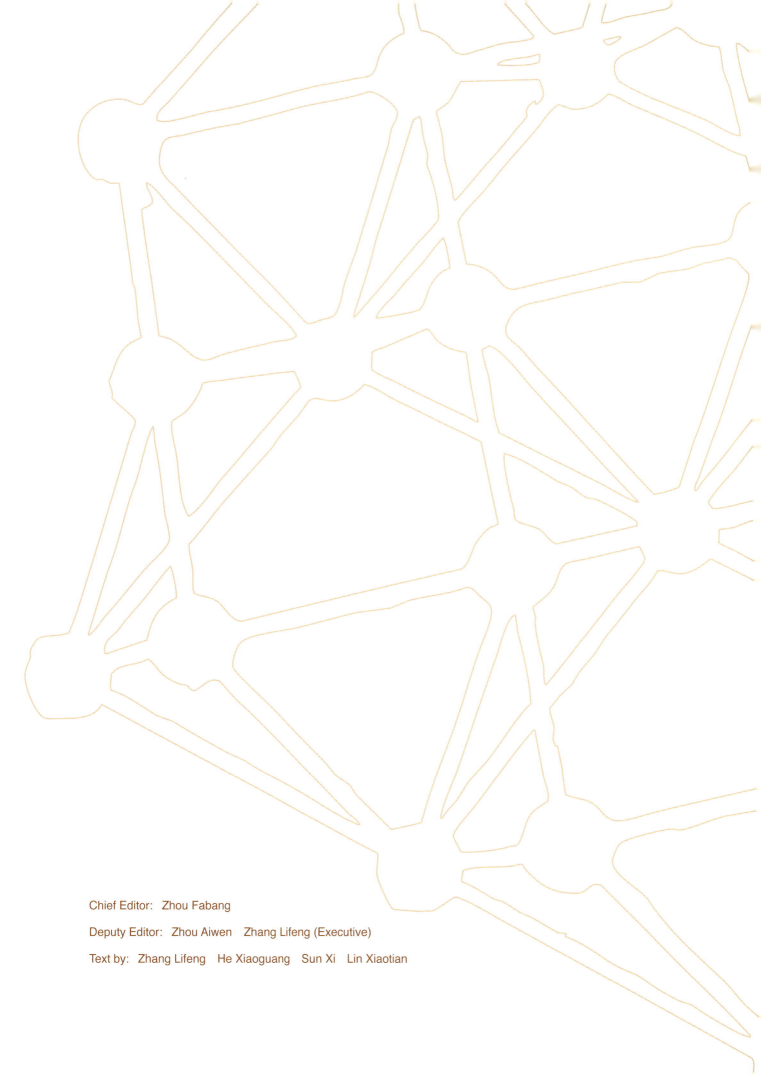

Chief Editor: Zhou Fabang

Deputy Editor: Zhou Aiwen   Zhang Lifeng (Executive)

Text by: Zhang Lifeng   He Xiaoguang   Sun Xi   Lin Xiaotian

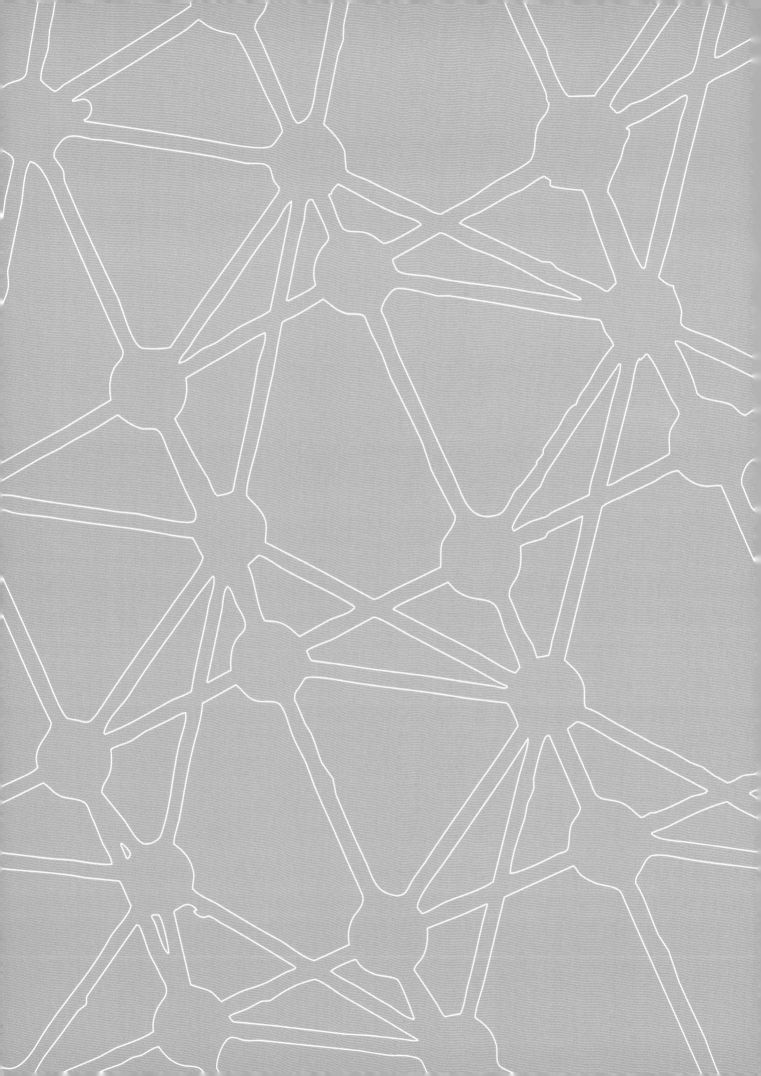

Preface

There is an English idiom ALL HIS GEESE ARE SWANS, which expresses one's particular love of his own belongings. In Chinese we have the similar sayings.

This is a kind of common and natural mentality of human beings. In many industries it has even become a long-standing tradition-workmen always cherish their own tools, which their lives lie on, and their own works, which they have devoted much to. Ancient Chinese carpenters used to clean up and wrap their axe in red cloth after using it. They cared for their tools as for their beloved relatives.

Construction professionals including designers and engineers are also such a group of people. Old measuring rulers and drawing pens, design drafts and structural drawings, reference books and specification collections, hand-made steel joints and large projects personally participating in-all of these are unforgettable memories and unique treasures. This kind of memory can inspire oneself and influence others at the same time, and it is the common wealth of the entire industry.

You may have known the story of ancient Chinese scientist Song Yingxing （宋应星）and his works *Tiangong Kaiwu* （天工开物）. After the 45-year-old Song failed his 6th imperial examination in 1631, he devoted himself to collecting technical knowledge of Chinese agriculture and handicrafts and completed his masterpiece after hard work of 3 years. This scientific masterpiece, *Tiangong Kaiwu*, was named the "Encyclopedia of Chinese Technologies" and had been translated into Japanese, French, German, English, and Russian texts, which profoundly benefitted technological development in various countries. In Japan, people were full of enthusiasm about the book and they even formed academic school to study it, which promoted the Meiji Restoration Movement and Japan's process of industrialization. This story tells the huge force of heritage for the development of the industry and society.

All construction designers and engineers should be proud of the profession and contribute to the development of the entire industry in our own way-SSM's collection of more than 1,000 pieces/sets by far is exactly from the donation and collection of industry masters, celebrities and CSCEC Science & Industry staffs. From this point of view, the construction of Steel Structure Museum is in the right season, and all its collections are extremely valuable.

I'm so pleased to be invited to write this preface and speak out what in my mind.

Chairman of CSCEC Science & Industry

Honorary Director of SSM

CONTENTS

Drawings and Manuscripts

Postals, Paper Notes and Souvenir

Others

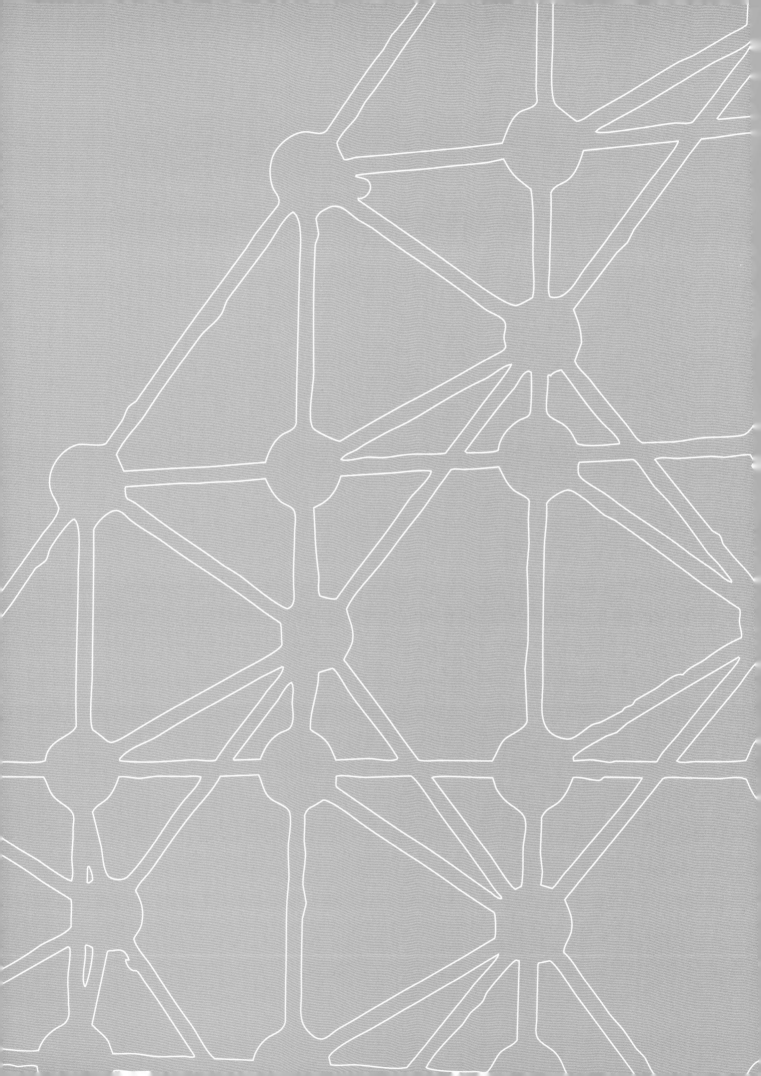

Components
Plates
and
Models

Iron Chain of Luding Bridge (partial)

Ancient

Iron

Piece length: 19 cm

Diameter of iron: 2.6 cm

Weight: 3.5 kg

Luding Bridge is located on the main traffic route from Sichuan to Xikang and Tibet. In 1705, in order to strengthen the connection with the Kangzang area, the Qing government decided to build a suspension bridge in the west of Luding city with a narrow river valley, low terrain and slow water flow, and completed it in the following year. The entire bridge consisted of 13 iron cables, of which 9 were bottom cables with a distance of 33 cm between them. Horizontal wooden boards were laid on these cables, and eight longitudinal wooden boards are laid on the horizontal ones as the bridge deck. The other four iron cables served as handrails for pedestrians. Each iron cable was 127.45 meters long and weighed about 2.5 tons. It was made of 800-900 flat rings. After the bridge was completed, only everyday regular traffic was allowed and the pedestrian number was limited to ensure safety.

These two iron chains were replaced during the overhaul of the Luding Bridge in 2005 and donated by Luding County Cultural Relics Administration.

Rivet of Eiffel Tower

———————————————

Modern

Steel

Gross length: 8 cm

Head diameter: 4.2 cm

Weight: 340 g

The Eiffel Tower is an iconic steel structure building located in the Champ de Mars in Paris. It was designed and constructed by the famous French architect and engineer Gustave Eiffel for World Expo 1889. The tower has a total height of 324 meters and uses 7,300 tons of steel and 12,000 metal components, which are connected by 2.5 million rivets.

This rivet was originally fixed on the Eiffel Tower between 1887 and 1889, and removed during later maintenance work. It is donated by the Societe d'Exploitation de la Tour Eiffel (SETE).

Steel Bars used for Factory Buildings of Qixin Cement Plant (4)

Modern

Steel

Length: 40 cm

Section size: 1~2 cm

Weight: 0.5~1.1 kg

Qixin Cement Plant is located in the downtown area of Tangshan, Hebei Province. It was built in 1889 by Mr. Tang Tingshu, a well-known comprador in modern China, an active participant in the Westernization Movement and the chief administer of the Kaiping Mining Bureau. China's first barrel of cement (measured by barrels of old cement) was produced in Qixin, and its "Ma"(horse) brand cement has won international awards many times. It had continuously produced for more than 120 years, until its No. 8 kiln stopped production in 2009.

These bamboo root-type steel bars were once used in the factory building of Qixin Cement Plant and are donated by China Cement Industry Museum.

Rivets of Waibaidu Bridge Shanghai (2)

Modern

Steel

The Waibaidu Bridge Shanghai is the first all-steel structure riveted bridge in China and the only remaining unequal-height truss structure bridge. Built under the auspices of the Ministry of Public Works of the Shanghai Public Concession at that time, it opened to traffic on January 20, 1908.

Waibaidu Bridge was fixed by about 160,000 rivets. Until today, except for the use in small-scale railway bridge construction, bridge riveting has basically disappeared. On April 6, 2008, as in its 100th anniversary, the bridge was removed from its original location and transported to Shanghai Shipyard for overhaul. Nearly 63,000 steel rivets were replaced in this overhaul, accounting for about 40% of the total.

These two rivets were replaced during the repair and donated by Shanghai Shipyard Co., Ltd.

Gross length: 3.5 cm

Head diameter: 3 cm

Weight: 80 g

Gross length: 6 cm

Head diameter: 3.5 cm

Weight: 220 g

Suspender Cable of Golden Gate Bridge (partial)

Contemporary

Steel

Length: 11 cm

Diameter: appr. 7.5 cm

Weight: 2.2 kg

This piece is an excessive section of the steel cables of the Golden Gate Bridge and donated by Mr. Li Renge.

The Golden Gate Bridge was completed in 1937 and is one of the most famous steel truss suspension bridges in the world. It is famous for the novel structure and extraordinary appearance. The giant steel towers on the north and south sides of the bridge are 342 meters high. The tower tops are connected by two main steel cables with a diameter of 92.7 centimeters and a weight of 24,500 tons. The weight of the roadway is hung from 250 pairs of vertical suspender ropes, which are attached to two main cables. The two ends of the cable extend to the shore and are anchored in the rock. The weight of the entire bridge deck is shared between the two towers via suspension cables without any support in the middle.

Each cable is made of 27,572 strands, and the total length of the steel cables reaches 130,000 kilometers. The "aggregation" method is used because it is impossible to manufacture a long and thick steel cable alone. More importantly, if a single cable was applied, it might mean catastrophic consequences once an accident occurs. Tens of thousands of thin steel bars will make maintenance and accident rescue easier.

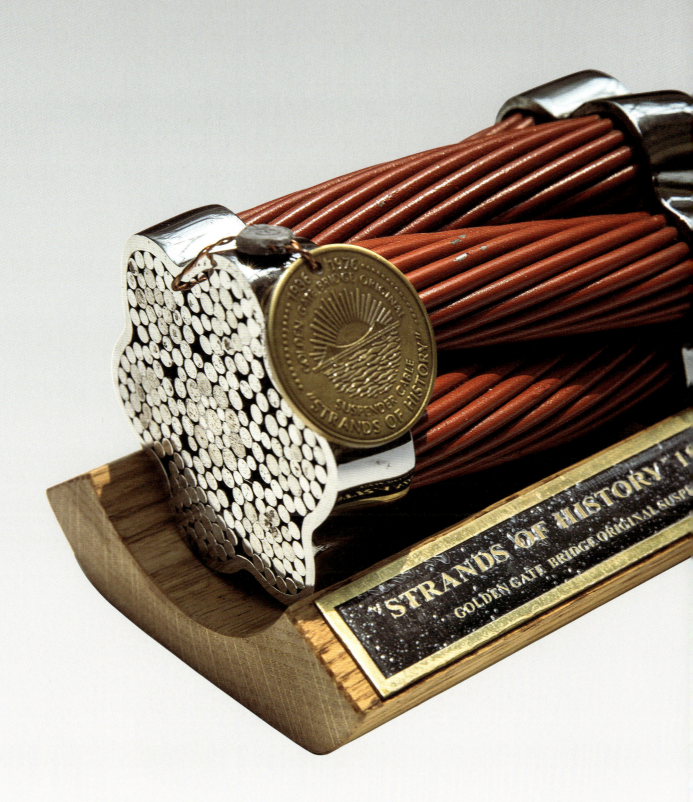

Rivet of Golden Gate Bridge

Contemporary

Steel

Gross length: 10 cm

Head diameter: 4 cm

Weight: 370 g

This rivet was produced for the construction of the Golden Gate Bridge. Today the iconic international orange color on its head is clearly identifiable.

It was a huge project: a total of about 1.2 million rivets were used to construct the Golden Gate Bridge. The designer of the bridge and his teammates used the most advanced bridge construction technology at that time and spent 4 years fixing the rivets and hanging cables. There is another interesting story about the Golden Gate Bridge rivets: On the day of the completion of the bridge in 1937, the architects came up with an idea and hoped to use a pure gold rivet to end this huge project. Unfortunately, the gold rivet was too soft and broke into the water before it was riveted. So Edward Stanley, the worker who had drilled the first rivet for the bridge, had to pick up the drill bit and unscrew the gold rivet.   People are enthusiastic about completion celebrations   because of such episodes.

It is donated by Mr. Li Renge.

Welded Spherical Joint Model

Contemporary

Steel

Gross length: 30 cm

Gross width: 28 cm

Gross height: 25 cm

Weight: 2.8 kg

Welded spherical joint is a node made by welding two hemispheres into a hollow ball, and then directly welding steel pipes with the ball together. It has the advantages of simple structure, clear force, and convenient connection. Welded spherical joint is highly adaptable. For all types of grids-regardless the span and the size of the applied load- the joints can all be applied when the nets are round steel pipes.

Welded spherical joint was developed by Professor Liu Xiliang of Tianjin University during 1964 to 1966. The first application project was Tianjin Science Museum. This model is donated by Professor Liu.

Space Truss Structure of Welded Spherical Joints Model

Contemporary

Steel

Gross length: 33 cm

Gross width: 21.5 cm

Gross height: 5 cm

Weight: 800 g

This model is a grid structure composed of welded spherical joints. It has the characteristics of large span, high strength, light weight, beautiful appearance, and no need for support. Grid structure is widely used in various circumstances including sports halls, hotels, restaurants and entertainment venues.

This model was donated by Professor Liu Xiliang, the developer of welded spherical joint.

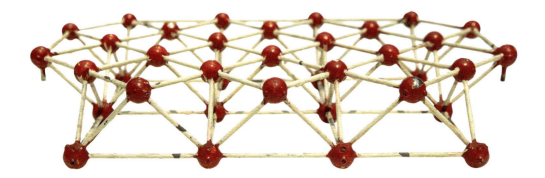

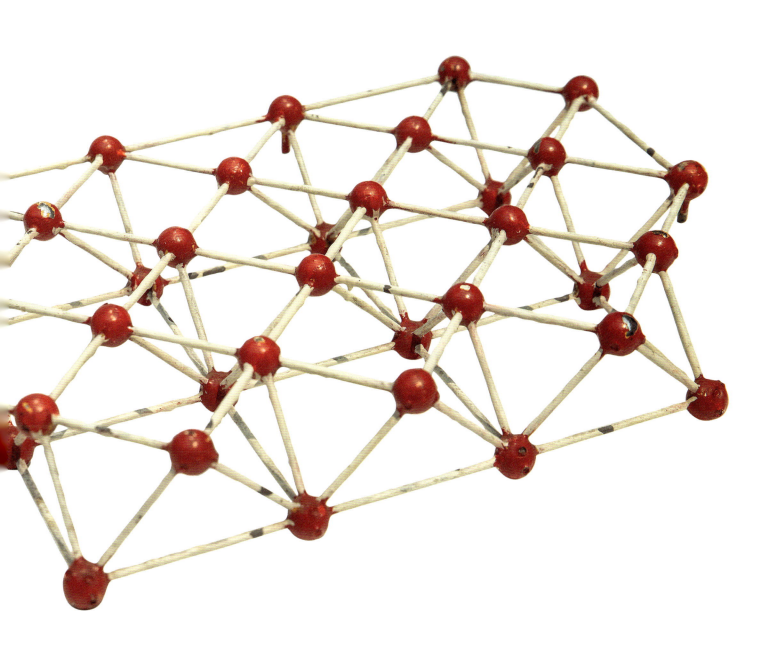

Steel Member of WTC

Contemporary
Steel
Gross length: 2.48 m
Gross width: 1.72 m
Gross height: 0.83 m
Weight: appr. 3 tons

This huge steel member is the wreckage left after the North Tower of the World Trade Center collapsed in the terrorist attacks of September 11, 2001. It was originally an octagonal part of the antenna at the top of the North Tower.

The WTC North and South Towers were successively completed in the early 1970s, and the North Tower was retrofitted with a 110-meter antenna in 1978. By the antenna and the radio and television transmitters located on the 110th floor, the North Tower sent almost all television signals in New York city and signals from four radio stations.

After the 9/11 terrorist attacks, more than 1.6 million tons of wreckage were removed from the original WTC site, at least 400,000 of which were steel. Most of them were sold through auctions for recycling and steelmaking, while people were also allowed to apply for them for "historical, memorial or educational purposes". Upon written application, the owner of the World Trade Center, the Port Authority of New York and New Jersey, donated this collection, one of the masterpieces of Steel Structure Museum.

Baosteel Weathering Steel Sample

Contemporary

Steel

Length: 34 cm

Width: 34 cm

Thickness: 2 cm

Weight: 30 kg

Weathering steel, often referred to by the genericized trademark COR-TEN steel and sometimes written without the hyphen as corten steel, is a group of steel alloys which were developed to eliminate the need for painting, and form a stable rust-like appearance after several years' exposure to weather.

This piece, with model number Q500qNHE, is a weathering steel sample produced and donated by Baosteel China.

Steel Tie Rod of Macau Tower

Contemporary

Steel

Length: 72.5 cm

Weight: 1.2 kg

The Macau Tower was completed in 2001 with a height of 338 meters. It ranks 21st among the world's tallest independent sightseeing towers and is a member of the World Federation of Great Towers (WFGT).

Its sightseeing tower is a six-story, tapered, stable structural system consisting of radial beams, hoop beams and columns. Above it is a two-story cantilever steel beam with a grid panel. The entire tower has used about 1,400 steel members including columns, beams and supports. The largest member is 16 meters long and weighs nearly 2 tons.

This piece is the first tie rod manufactured for the sightseeing tower and donated by Mr. Chen Wenge.

Steel for the Bird's Nest Project

Contemporary

Steel

Lenth: 20 cm

Width: 4 cm

Thickness: 1.1 cm

Weight: 1 kg

This piece is a low-alloy and high-strength Q460E steel plate specially developed and produced by Wuyang Iron and Steel Company for the "Bird's Nest" project of the 2008 Beijing Olympics. Q represents the strength of the steel, 460 indicates that it will undergo plastic deformation only when the strength reaches 460 MPa. 460 MPa is equivalent to 4540 standard atmospheric pressure, while the strength of ordinary steel is only 235 MPa. E represents the electromagnetic performance as super.

In the Chinese national standard, the maximum thickness of the Q460 series steel is 100 mm, while the thickness of the steel plate required to build the Bird's Nest reaches 110 mm. After several trials, Wuyang Company successfully trial-produced the above steel plates in May 2005, which ensured the smooth construction of the project. The technical requirements of Q460E steel plate reached the highest level of alloyed high-strength steel at that time, creating the only domestic and world first record, and realizing all the "Bird's Nest" steel "made in China".

In January 2006, 2008 commemorative plates made of the above-mentioned steel were released. Steel Structure Museum houses the 89th of them.

It is donated by Mr. Zhou Hailin.

Anode-sacrificed Zinc Block

Contemporary

Zinc

Gross length: 42 cm

Gross width: 10 cm

Weight: 2.9 kg

A galvanic anode, or sacrificial anode, is the main component of a galvanic cathodic protection (CP) system used to protect buried or submerged metal structures from corrosion. They are made from a metal alloy with a more "active" voltage (more negative reduction potential / more positive electrochemical potential) than the metal of the structure. The difference in potential between the two metals means that the galvanic anode corrodes, so that the anode material is consumed in preference to the structure.

The sacrificial anode consumes quickly, and the installation position and method must be easy to replace. Common materials include magnesium, magnesium alloy, zinc, zinc alloy, and aluminum alloy. This collection is a metal zinc block that has been used as a sacrificial anode, and it has been consumed by the oxidation reaction.

It is donated by Jotun China.

Gold Medal Works of WorldSkills (3)

Contemporary

Steel

These containers are gold medal winners of welding at the 3 WorldSkills Competitions from 2015 to 2019, the gold standard of skills excellence in the world.

WorldSkills organises the world championships of vocational skills, and is held every two years in different parts of the world. It promotes the benefits of and need for skilled trade professionals. China has won 3 gold, 1 silver and 1 bronze in welding since it became a WorldSkills member in 2010.

The works are donated by China Engineering Construction Welding Association, CECWA.

Winner of WorldSkills São Paulo 2015

by Zeng Zhengchao

Gross length: 47.5cm

Gross width: 28.7cm

Gross height: 39.2cm

Weight: 40kg

Winner of WorldSkills Abu Dhabi 2017

by Ning Xianhai

Gross length: 49.1cm

Gross width: 26.2cm

Gross height: 38.2cm

Weight: 55kg

Winner of WorldSkills Kazan 2019 by Zhao Fubo

Gross length: 45cm

Gross width: 25.5cm

Gross height: 41cm

Weight: 45kg

Robot-welded Steel Node

Contemporary

Steel

Gross length: 65 cm

Gross width: 27 cm

Gross height: 27 cm

Weight: 20 kg

This is a steel node welded by robot, and donated by CSCEC Science and Industry Guangdong Manufacturing Base. It is usually a component of a steel pipe truss or grid, in different shape and size.

An industrial robot is a multi-purpose, reprogrammable automatic controlled manipulator with three or more axes and used in the field of industrial automation. In order to adapt to different uses, the mechanical interface of the last axis of the robot is usually a connecting flange, which can be used to connect different end effectors. A welding robot is a tool that attaches a welding gun and other tools to the final shaft flange to enable it to perform welding operations.

Robot welding has obvious advantages. On one hand, it can stabilize and improve the welding quality and reflect the welding quality in the form of data. On the other hand, it can improve labor productivity, improve the labor intensity of workers, and reduce the requirements for workers' operating technology.

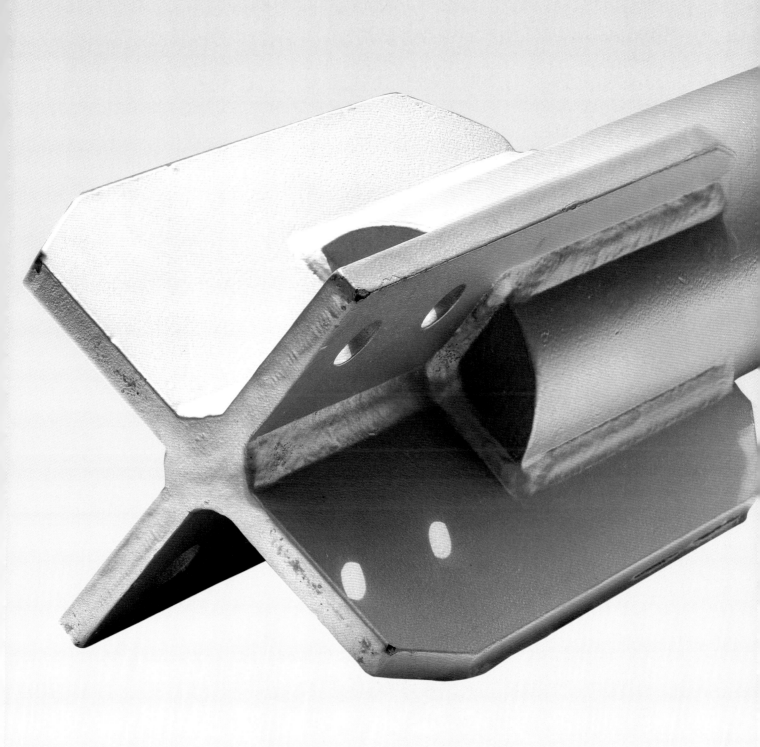

Cast Steel Node

Contemporary

Steel

Gross length: 52 cm

Gross width: 35 cm

Gross height: 33 cm

Weight: 98 kg

This is a steel node manufactured by casting, and donated by Jiangsu Yongyi Cast Pipes Co., LTD.

Steel casting is a specialized form of casting involving various types of steel. Steel castings are used when cast irons cannot deliver enough strength or shock resistance. Examples of items that are steel castings include: hydroelectric turbine wheels, forging presses, gears, railroad truck frames, valve bodies, pump casings, mining machinery, marine equipment, turbocharger turbines and engine cylinder blocks.

Rotary Damper

Contemporary

Steel

Width: 15.5 cm

Thickness: 4 cm

Gross height: 14 cm

Weight: 600 g

Rotary dampers provide an invisible yet valuable service as a maintenance-free machine element to allow controlled deceleration of rotary or linear movements. They are often necessary to make careful opening and closing of small lids, compartments and drawers possible. This model is donated by Nikken Design of Japan, and its prototype is applied to the spiral tower of MODE Academy in Nagoya.

3D-Printed Steel Node

Contemporary

Steel

Gross width: 10 cm

Gross height: 14 cm

Diameter: 5.4 cm

Weight: 500 g

This is a steel node manufactured by 3D printing process, and purchased from Arup Netherlands.

3D printing process builds a three-dimensional object from a computer-aided design model, usually by successively adding material layer by layer, which is why it is also called additive manufacturing. The term "3D printing" covers a variety of processes in which material is joined or solidified under computer control to create a three-dimensional object, with material being added together, typically layer by layer. In the 1990s, 3D-printing techniques were considered suitable only for the production of functional or aesthetic prototypes and a more appropriate term for it was rapid prototyping. As of 2019, the precision, repeatability, and material range have increased to the point that some 3D-printing processes are considered viable as an industrial-production technology, whereby the term additive manufacturing can be used synonymously with "3D printing". One of the key advantages of 3D printing is the ability to produce very complex shapes or geometries, and a prerequisite for producing any 3D printed part is a digital 3D model or a CAD file.

It was purchased from Arup Netherlands.

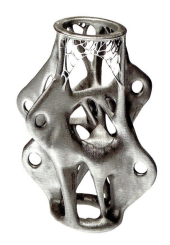

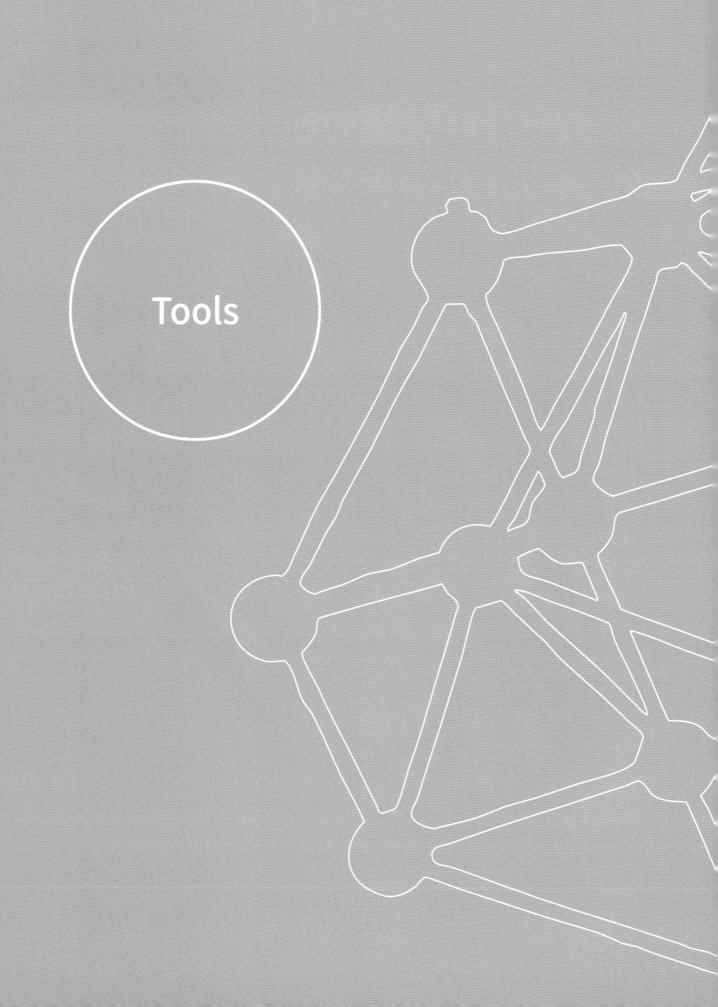

Tools

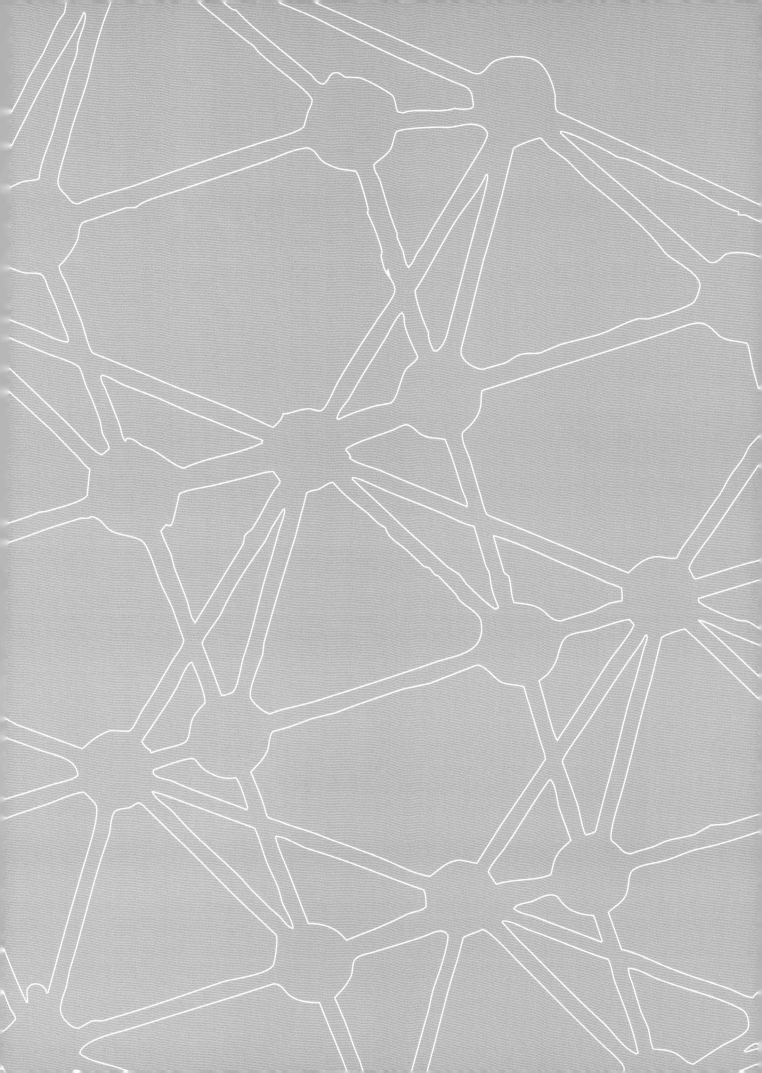

Copper Hammer of Kunming-Haiphong Railway

Modern
Copper
Gross length: 29 cm
Gross width: 15 cm
Weight: 1.5 kg

The Kunming–Haiphong railway is an 855 km railway built by France during 1904 to 1910, connecting Haiphong, Vietnam with Kunming, Yunnan province, China. The section within China from Kunming to Hekou is known as the Kunming–Hekou railway, and is 466 km long. The railway was built with 1,000 mm gauge due to the mountainous terrain along the route. Currently it is the only main line in China using 1,000 mm gauge.

This hammer, made of heavy copper, was collected from the Yunnan Railway Museum.

Carbide Lamp of the Wujiazhai Bridge

Modern

Copper

Gross height: 19.5 cm

Base dimeter: 6 cm

Weight: 580 g

Carbide lamps, or acetylene gas lamps, are simple lamps that produce and burn acetylene which is created by the reaction of calcium carbide with water. Acetylene gas lamps were used to illuminate buildings, as lighthouse beacons, and as headlights on motor-cars and bicycles. Portable acetylene gas lamps, worn on the hat or carried by hand, were widely used in mining in the early twentieth century.

During the construction of the Kunming-Haiphong Railway, the natural conditions were harsh and the construction equipment was simple. Carbide lamps provided great help for night and pothole operations.

This carbide lamp, made of heavy copper, was collected from the Yunnan Railway Museum.

Plumb Bob

Modern

Copper

Gross length: 7 cm

Maximum diameter: 3.5 cm

Weight: 200 g

The verticality correction is particularly important in the field of steel structure installation. A plumb bob, or plummet, is a weight, usually with a pointed tip on the bottom, suspended from a string and used as a vertical reference line, or plumb-line. It is a precursor to the spirit level and used to establish a vertical or horizontal datum.

It is donated by Mr. Zhang Kaiming.

Chain Block

_____

Contemporary

Alloyed steel

Gross length: 3 m

Weight: 20 kg

A Chain Block (also known as a hand chain hoist) is a mechanism used to lift and lower heavy loads using a chain. Chain blocks contain two wheels which the chain is wound around. When the chain is pulled, it winds around the wheels and begins to lift the item that is attached to the rope or chain via a hook. Chain Blocks can also be attached to lifting slings or chain bags to lift the load more evenly.

It is donated by CSCEC Science and Industry Southern China Branch.

Shackles (2)

B-type Shackle
Contemporary
Steel
Steel diameter: 2 cm
Loop ID: 6 cm
Weight: 1.6 kg

D-type Shackle
Contemporary
Steel
Steel diameter: 2 cm
Loop ID: 3 cm
Weight: 1 kg

A shackle is a usually U-shaped fastening device secured by a bolt or pin through holes in the end of the two arms, which is used for connection between ropes and objects in steel structure installation and lifting operations.

They are donated by Mr. Zhu Guangjian.

B-type Shackle

D-type Shackle

Monitoring Sensors of Qiantang River Bridge (3)

Contemporary

Steel

As for steel bridges in use especially those long-span bridges, damage will occur due to the effects of vehicle load and temperature, as well as the shrinkage and creep of concrete. Installing a detection system can monitor the changes in the bearing capacity of the bridge in real time, detect problems in time, and provide assistance for bridge maintenance.

At the end of 2012, the Qiantang River Bridge established a safety monitoring system. The bridge was equipped with 6 dynamic strain test sections, which were located in each span. Here are three sensors that were replaced when the bridge monitoring system was upgraded in March 2016. Among them, the cylindrical is 891-4A vibration pickup sensor and the rectangular is dynamic strain sensor.

They are donated by China Railway Bridge & Tunnel Technologies Co., LTD.

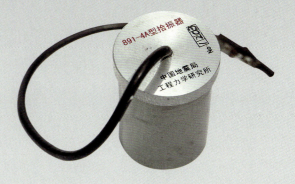

Length: 5 cm

Diameter: 4 cm

Wire length: 26 cm

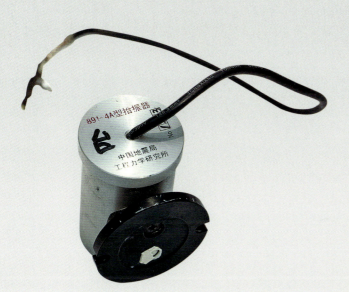

Length: 6 cm

Diameter: 4 cm

Wire length: 30 cm

Gross length: 13 cm

Gross width: 4 cm

Gross height: 3.5 cm

Wire length: 14 cm

Books
Newspapers
and
Magazines

Specifications for Steel Railway Bridges

Modern

Paper

1/16

77 pages

This specification was formulated by the Ministry of Communications of the Republic of China, approved by the State Council, and promulgated by Order No. 117 of the Ministry on November 6, 1922. It is bilingual, as the first half in English and the second half in Traditional Chinese, and introduces construction method and other regulations including general rules, bridge deck, load and stress, the control of each part, design details, materials, monolithic test, working method, lacquer, etc., which is a precious testimony to historical situation of China's railway construction at that time.

It is donated by Mr. Chen Zhenming.

交通部製訂

國有鐵路鋼橋規範書

---

shall be securely held in position; furthermore, they shall be arra...
ed that the sliding surfaces thereof cannot become clogged by...

Bridges on an inclined grade without pin shoes shall...
sole plates bevelled so that the masonry and expansion surface...
be level.

Fixed Bearings

87. Fixed bearings shall be firmly anchored to the ma...

Pier-Members.

88. Spans of 30 meters (100 feet) and over shall prefera...
upon hinged or disc bearings, which shall be constructed...
distribute the load evenly over the entire bearing. Bed-plates...
castings, or they may be of rolled steel.

Anchor-Bolts

89. Anchor-bolts shall not be less than 30 mm. (one a...
quarter (1¼ inches) in diameter.

Anchorage

90. Anchor-bolts for viaduct-towers and similar str...
shall be long enough to engage a mass of masonry weighing...
than one and one-half (1½) times the amount of the net upli...

Camber

91. Trusses shall be cambered, either by increasing th...
of the top chords 1 mm. per meter (⅛ inch per 10 feet); or b...
difying the length of member that the floor-line will be stra...
the bridge is fully loaded, and the length of diagonal membe...
calculated accordingly.

The amount of camber of the unloaded bridge when erec...
shown on the working drawings, and also the amount of init...
employed during temporary erection at the manufacturer's w...

25

Materials

Steel

92. Steel shall be made by the Open-hearth process.

Properties

93. The chemical and physical properties of steel shall conform to the following limits:—

Elements considered.	Structural Steel.	Rivet Steel.	Cast Steel.
Phosphorus, max. Basic.	0.05 per cent	0.05 per cent	0.05 per cent
do do Acid.	0.06 per cent	0.04 per cent	0.08 per cent
Sulphur, do	0.05 per cent	0.04 per cent	0.05 per cent
Ultimate tensile strength, in kgs. per mm.²	38.5 to 45.5 $\left\{\begin{array}{l}55,000\ \text{to}\\65,000\ \text{lbs.}\\ \text{per sq. in.}\end{array}\right\}$	31.5 to 38.5 $\left\{\begin{array}{l}45,000\ \text{to}\\55,000\ \text{lbs.}\\ \text{per sq. in.}\end{array}\right\}$	45.5 (65,000 lbs. per sq. in.) minimum
Yield point, in kgs. per mm.² minimum	21 (30,000 lbs. per in.²)	17.5 (25,000 lbs. per in.²)	23 (33,000 lbs. per in.²)
Elongation, minimum percentage in 200 mm. (8 in.), Fig. I	$\dfrac{1654}{\text{Ultimate tensile strength}}$ $\left\{\dfrac{1,500,000}{\text{Ult. tensile strength in lbs. per in.}^2}\right\}$		15
Elongation, min, percentage in 50 mm. (2 in.), Fig. II	22		
Cold bends without fracture.	180° flat	180° flat	90°, d = 3t

in which d = diameter of pin.

t = thickness of specimen.

Steel and Timber Structures (English)

Modern

Paper

1/32

695 pages

Published in 1923, this book is an English reference book on the design and construction of modern major engineering structures. The authors are George A. Hool and W. S. Kinne, professors of structural engineering at the University of Wisconsin, USA. It has 695 pages in 11 sections, covering construction, roof trusses, short-span steel bridges, wooden bridges and trestle bridges, steel tanks, chimneys, structural steel details, steel structure manufacturing, steel structure installation, steel Structural estimates and materials, and is appended with professional specifications, e.g. the American Railway Engineering Association's General Specifications for Steel Bridges.

It is donated by Mr. Xu Ziming.

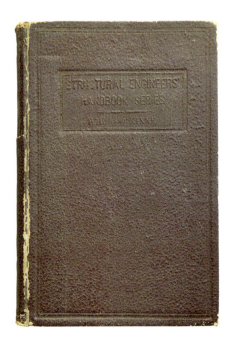

is well to design the connections of girders to columns, and joists to columns, relatively strong, providing continuity across the columns. Details of such connections are discussed in the volume on Structural Members and Connections.

42e. Connections to Walls.—All girders and joists entering masonry walls should rest upon steel or iron bearing plates, well painted. An air space should be left around the ends of the joists and girders. In order to allow the ends of the timbers to fall without pulling the walls over in case of fire, the ends of girders or joists into the walls are usually cut back, as in Fig. 172. For tying the girders and joists into the walls, iron or steel anchors are used, as illustrated in Fig. 172. These anchors should be approximately $1/4 \times 1\frac{1}{2}$-in. straps, one end forged into a

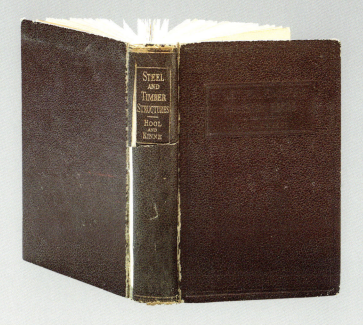

Fig. 172.—Details of connection—timber joists to brick walls.   Fig. 173.—Van Dorn box anchor.   Fig. 174.—"Ideal" wall box.

lug to fit into a notch in the upper side of girder. The portion within the wall may be bonded into the masonry. Sometimes an anchor consisting of a round rod is passed through the wall, and is fitted with an exterior ornamental cast-iron washer on the outside. The other end of the rod may be forged into a flat strap with a lug as before.

Every girder should be anchored into the wall. In the case of joists, at least every sixth joist should be so anchored. Building ordinances usually specify in detail the size and arrangement of wall anchors.

Joists, closely spaced, entering a masonry wall weaken the walls. Further, unless very careful inspection is maintained, one can never be certain that proper air spaces will be left around the timbers entering the wall. For this reason, there have been developed wall boxes, made of malleable iron, steel, and cast iron, which insure an air space around the joist or girder, and at the same time allow the timber to be self-releasing in case of fire. The tie between timber and wall is secured by a lug on the base of the anchor which engages a notch on the under side of joist or girder. Typical box anchors are shown in Figs. 173 to 176 inclusive. Figure 177 shows a Duplex wall plate.

A third method for support of girders and joists is the wall hanger shown in Figs. 178 and 179. With the wall hanger, no hole is left in the wall. Since the joists and girders with this device extend only to the inner surface of the wall, a saving in timber is made. Since lumber comes in lengths of multiples of 2 ft. only, the use of the wall hanger as compared to the box anchor may mean a saving, in many cases, of 2 ft. in the length of timber—a very considerable item.

42f. Typical Floor Bay Design.—The following example will illustrate the necessary computations for designing the joists and girders of a typical floor bay. The framing plan of the bay is shown in Fig. 180.

Fig. 175.—Lane wrought steel wall box.   Fig. 176.—Duplex wall box.   Fig. 177.—Duplex wall plate.

Data: Office floor; partitions 2×4 in., plastered both sides, 12 ft. high; flooring double, under floor rough 1×6 in., upper floor 1×4 in., T & G; ceiling plastered; joists 16 in. on centers; live load for joists, 60 lb. per sq. ft.; ceiling for girders, 48 lb. per sq. ft.; live load for stairs, 75 lb. per sq. ft.

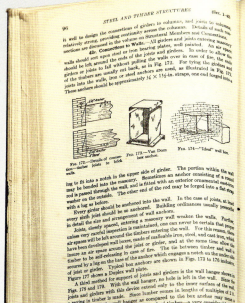

Fig. 178.—Duplex wall hanger.   Fig. 179.—"Fails" joist hanger.

For approximate dead load, call flooring 2 in. thick at 3 lb. per board foot; assume joists 2×16 in.—16 in. on centers; allow 1 lb. per sq. ft. for bridging; assume plaster ceiling weight 5 lb. per sq. ft.; assume girder weight as 2 lb. per sq. ft.

Timber: Douglas fir, dense structural grade, all timbers to be taken as 8181E,[1] working stress 1,800 lb. per sq. in. in flexure and 175 lb. in horizontal shear.

Loadings:	Joists	Girders
Flooring	6	6
Joists	6	6
Bridging	1	1
Ceiling	5	5
Girder	0	2
Total dead load	18	20
Live load	60	48
Total dead and live load	78 lb. per sq. ft.	68 lb. per sq. ft.

[1] Surfaced one side and one edge.

7

Commemorative Journal of the Start of Qiantang River Bridge

Modern

Paper

1/16

115 pages

Construction of the Qiantang River Bridge started on November 11, 1934. A commemorative journal was compiled to commemorate this important moment by the Engineering Office, which was headed by Mr. Mao Yisheng.

The journal records a large number of people and events related to the bridge, including the start-up ceremony arrangements, speeches by important guests from the Ministry of Communications and the Zhejiang Province government, a list of contractors and their representatives, media reports, engineering descriptions and technical materials, personal photos and engineering drawings, which are important materials for understanding and studying the project.

It is donated by Mr. Liu Qingquan.

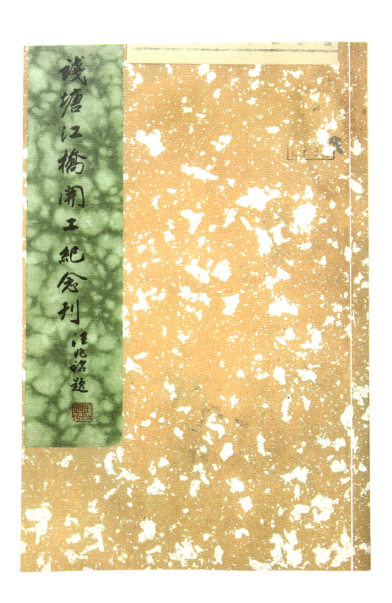

錢塘江橋開工紀念刊　汪地略題

Steel Construction

Modern

Paper

1/32

471 pages

Steel Construction, originally written by Henry J. Burt, translated by Xu Zhichan in 1940, is the tenth volume in the Civil Engineering Series published by the American Institute of Technology. It is divided into 5 sections and 34 chapters, which comprehensively introduces the steel structure and provides important references for the architectural design of the time.

It is donated by Mr. Chen Zhenming.

Steel Roof Design

Modern
Paper
1/32
194 pages

This is a textbook for vocational schools in the Republic of China period, edited by Zhou Songwen, published by the Commercial Press in 1940. With 194 pages in total, it is divided into 4 chapters, including general introduction, the form of roof trusses, burden of roof trusses and roof truss design, and accompanied by a series of schedules.

At that time, the Commercial Press was the leader in editing and printing textbooks at all levels in primary and secondary schools. According to the commission of the Ministry of Education of the National Government, it organized vocational textbook committees, solicited self-edited handouts from vocational schools in various provinces and cities nationwide, selected and printed them for selection by vocational schools. This book draws on relevant foreign materials and makes a relatively complete description of the design of steel roof trusses.

It is donated by Mr. Zhang Kaiming.

應力，如第六表中之第六行。

最大應力　各種擔負之應力旣已全部求出，仰當將此接照前述之四種情形相併合，以求結合之應力，如第六表中之

圖十九

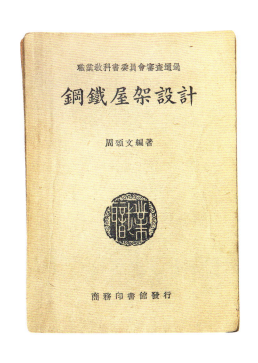

職業教科書委員會審查適用

鋼鐵屋架設計

周頌文編著

商務印書館發行

Structural Theory (English)

Modern
Paper
1/32
368 pages

    This is an English textbook on structural theory related to trusses, rigid frames and space frames. It was published in 1942 by Hale Sutherland, Professor of Civil Engineering at Lehigh University, and Harry Lake Bowman, Professor of Civil Engineering at Drexel Institute of Technology. There are totally 368 pages and 12 chapters, including reaction and stress, graphic statics, roof trusses, trusses and beam bridges, long-span bridges, lateral supports and portals, slopes and deflections, rigid frames, high-rise building frames wind stress, uncertain truss, secondary stress, space frame, etc.

    It is donated by Professor Liu Xiliang.

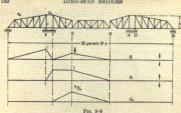

Fig. 5-9

5-5) are indeterminate. The latter would be identical in arrangement with the Beaver bridge (Fig. 5-7) were it not that a horizontal force acting on the suspended span develops horizontal reactions on both main piers.

The computation of reactions is illustrated in the following example.

Example 5-2. Draw influence lines for the vertical reactions at 6 and 7 of the bridge in Fig. 5-9.

Solution. Load at panel point 10. The solution is much simplified by first taking the suspended span as a free body. It is obvious that no reactions are developed acting on this free body except when it carries a load and, consequently, only then does it bring load to either suspended span. It follows at once that each shore structure with its anchor and cantilever arms is entirely independent, carrying any load upon it without help from the other: a load on one does not affect the other.

For a load at point 10 there is no stress in the hanger at 16 and the shear in panel 19-20 being zero, V_{19} must be zero. Considering as a free body the right-hand shore structure, application of the conditions of equilibrium makes it plain that the reactions at points 20 and 26 are also zero. Considering the left shore structure, $V_7 = 1 \uparrow$ ($S_{6-7} = 0$); to balance the clockwise couple $1 \times 3\,p$ there must be developed $V_6 = \frac{1}{3} \downarrow$, $V_6 = \frac{1}{3} \uparrow$. The rest of the influence line may now be drawn very simply with no computations. The same applies to the second influence line, that for V_7.

Example 5-3. Draw influence line for the stress in bar a of the structure shown in Fig. 5-9.

Solution. The free body chosen was the cantilever arm supported by the reaction at 7 and the two horizontal bar stresses. In problems of this type remember that the load travels on a floor system and brings loads to the truss only at panel points.

Example 5-4. What are the reactions on the structure shown in Fig. 5-10 due to the load shown?

Solution. The equations available for use are (1) $\Sigma M = 0$, (2) $\Sigma H = 0$, (3) $\Sigma V = 0$, (4) $M_8 = 0$, (5) $S_{3-4} = 0$; there are five unknowns and the structure is statically determinate. Probably the simplest procedure is to make use of these equations one by one and either evaluate any reaction element directly or express it in terms of another unknown so that there results a free body with all the unknowns expressed in terms of one of them.

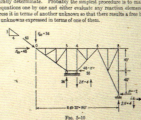

Fig. 5-10

The 60-kip load is resolved into H and V components: since $S_{3-4} = 0$, $V_3 = 36 \uparrow$. Calling the unknown horizontal component at L_8, H, $V_8 = 2\,H$ since $M_8 = 0$; also $H_4 = 48 - H$ acting to the left since $\Sigma H = 0$ and $V_4 = 2\,H$ down since $S_{3-4} = 0$. This second use of this condition is equivalent to using $\Sigma V = 0$, and there remains only $\Sigma M = 0$ for determining H. The most convenient center of moments is at U_6 since it eliminates three terms of the moment equation, giving

$$-36 \times 60 - 2\,H \times 40 + (48 - H)40 = 0$$

whence $H = -2$, that is, acting in direction opposite to that assumed.

5-4. Determinate and Indeterminate Structures. The preceding articles of this chapter give methods for determining whether or not the structures here treated are determinate as regards outer forces. Since, however, these structures are not rigid, as that term is defined in Art. 1-8, they will not be composed of $2\,n - 3$ bars, n being the number of joints. Since each joint represents a concurrent coplanar force system in equilibrium, as before, $2\,n$ independent equations may be written. For a structure to be statically determinate as regards both outer and inner forces the combined number of reaction components, r, and bar stresses, b, must equal the number of equations. That is, $b + r = 2\,n$, or

$$b = 2\,n - r$$

and a structure that is both stable and statically determinate as regards *inner* forces will follow this rule.

History of Wuhan Bridge Projects (replica)

Modern

Paper

Vertical: 30 cm

Horizontal: 21 cm

8 pages

History of Wuhan Bridge Projects is the work of bridge pioneer Mr. Li Wenji on the Wuhan Yangtze River Bridge construction plan. The full text is completed in 1948, and divided into 7 parts, including: the plan of Peking University, the plan of the former Ministry of Railways, the plan of the Qiantang River Bridge Engineering Office, and plan of the Preparation Committee, reviews of all plans, another design summary of the Yangtze River Bridge, and thoughts on the history of the plan, which have detailed the plans and history of different institutions on Wuhan Bridge from the beginning of the 20th century to the founding of the PRC.

It is donated by Ms. Tao Lei.

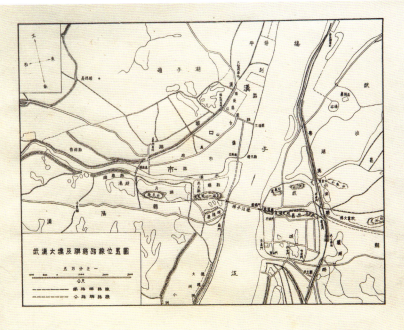

武漢大橋及聯絡路綫位置圖

五萬分之一

公尺

鐵路聯絡綫
公路聯絡綫

武漢大橋計劃之歷史　李文驥

武漢跨江建橋之議始於民國元年，詹天佑先生任川粵漢鐵路會辦時，曾準備測設建橋工程圖。

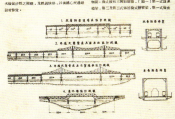

第一圖

北京大學之計劃

民國二年由北京大學教授德國籍專家葛 Professor Georg Muller 平漢鐵路土木工程師等十餘人規畫……

前鐵道部之計劃

民十七年冬鐵道部成立，聘德人怀德爾博士 Dr. J.A.L. Waddel……

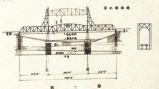

第二圖

Qiantang River Bridge

Contemporary
Paper
1/32
85 pages

Qiantang River Bridge is a monograph written by Mr. Mao Yisheng on the project. It was published in 1950 by China Science Books and Instruments Corporation and was one of its scientific pictorial series. The book is of 1/32 format and has 85 pages, which are divided into 5 chapters and various supporting materials.

The original manuscript was written by Mr. Mao during the bridge construction. At that time, the project attracted widespread attention from Chinese and foreigners. The Chinese Science Company published the manuscript in the "Science Pictorial" one by one as a systematic report. As a scientific popularization material, Mr. Mao minimized the use of terminology when writing, and omitted the contents of statistics and calculation formulas in order to meet the public's understanding.

It is donated by Mr. Xu Ziming.

錢塘江橋

茅以昇著

鋼，堅強得多，礅的混凝土內用鋼筋架緊，這梁與礅的重疊，便一律減輕了。在不明內情的人，站在浩瀚洶湧的錢塘江邊，遠看這細小的礅，細小的梁，或不悉要替過橋的人耽心，殊不知這些細小的東西裏面，卻蘊藏着絕大的威力呢！

鋼梁是用剪裁好的鋼料，一件一件地拼讓起來，用鉚釘聯繫成的。料是廠中做，橋是工地搭，如何能把這些材料，搭在江中形的礅上，便是所謂"安裝"工程的技術。這是與橋孔長度，江底深淺，水面高低，築礅次序，等等有密切關係的。普通有四種方法：(1)在水淺的地方，先搭木架，在架上拼裝鋼料，稱為"搭架法"；(2)如橋礅是從兩岸起，順序的向江中逐漸完成的，可從已裝好的梁上，一節一節向外挑出，直達到對邊的橋礅為止，稱為"懸臂法"；(3)懸橋過江，藉繩為根據，把鋼料吊起裝配，稱為"纜索法"；(4)在岸上將每橋孔的鋼料，鉚合成形，用浮船把這全梁運到兩礅間，整壁地落在礅上，稱為"浮運法"。前三種方法都是在江

圖35 鋼料堆棧

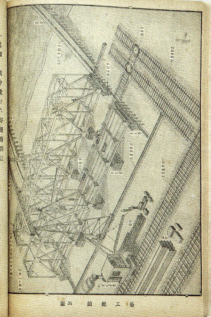

圖36 錢礅工場

The Draft Code of Steel Structure Design

Contemporary

Paper

1/32

82 pages

In order to meet the needs of large-scale construction, the Ministry of Construction and Engineering issued *The Draft Code of Steel Structure Design*(Regulation-4-54) in 1954, which was published by Construction Engineering Press one year after. The contents of the draft included the main principles, calculation methods, material properties and important structural requirements in the design of steel structures. There are 59 articles in total, divided into 11 chapters, and 4 reference materials attached.

This draft was prepared on the basis of the Steel Structure Design Standards and Technical Regulations promulgated by the Soviet Union in 1946, and it had been only tried out in limited fields. In 1956, the Ministry of Construction and Engineering translated and published the Steel Structure Design Standards and Technical Specifications promulgated by the Soviet Union in 1955 to replace Regulation -4-54. Therefore, this draft was not formally used.

It is donated by Professor Liu Xiliang.

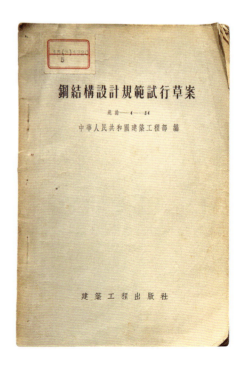

$$\frac{QS_{6P}}{J_{6P}\delta} \leqslant [\tau]$$

式中：φ_6 為按表十一或表十二採用的容許應力折減係數，鉚字梁中可採用 $W_{6P}=0.85W_{6P}$；

S_{6P} 為自驗算處至邊線部分截面全面積 對總 截面形心軸的靜矩。

鉚成工字梁受撓時的容許應力折減係數 φ_6

鉚成工字梁的折減係數 φ_6　　　　　表十一

l(公尺)	2.0	3.0	4.0	5.0	6.0	7.0	8.0	9.0
φ_6	0.98	0.94	0.89	0.82	0.71	0.61	0.54	0.48

鑄成及銲成工字梁受撓時的容許應力折減係數 φ_6

鑄成及銲成工字梁的折減係數 φ_6　　　　　表十二

$\dfrac{l}{b}$								
	20	30	40	50	60	70	80	90
10	1.00	1.00	1.00	1.00	1.00	1.00	1.00	1.00
15	0.99	0.97	0.96	0.96	0.95	0.95	0.95	
20	0.94	0.90	0.89	0.88	0.88	0.87	0.87	
25	0.90	0.85	0.77	0.71	0.68	0.66	0.65	
30	0.86	0.68	0.57	0.52	0.49	0.47	0.46	
35	0.79	0.58	0.46	0.41	0.38	0.36	0.35	
40	0.69	0.47	0.38	0.33	0.31	0.29	0.28	0.37

註：(1)上表中 l 為梁的跨度或受壓翼緣支撐點的間距；
b 為受壓翼緣寬度；
h 為梁的高度；
δ_1 為受壓翼緣的厚度（包括翼緣角鋼及蓋板的厚度）

(2)有蓋板（或型鋼）的受壓翼緣對稱於覆板時，應取蓋板（或型鋼）的寬度為翼緣的寬度 b；

(3)梁的受壓翼緣不對稱於覆板時，其折減係數 φ_6 應根據受壓翼緣寬度 b 算出之值後，按上表最末一行 $h/\delta_1 \geqslant 100$ 內採用；

(4)僅用翼緣角鋼與覆板 銲成的工字梁，當 $\frac{h}{\delta} > 3\frac{\delta_1}{\delta}$ 時，其折減係數 φ_6 應按上表求得的數值乘以 $=1.1-0.01\frac{l}{b}$ 的值。

式中：
δ 為腹板厚度，δ_1 為角鋼厚度。

第 39 條 構件的容許長細比 λ 為其在某不面內的壓屈長度 l_0 與其截面在同平面內旋幅 γ 的比。

受壓構件的長細比不得超過表十三的規定。

受壓構件的容許長細比　　　　　表十三

結構名稱	構件類別	最大長細比
桁架	弦桿及與支承點結合的各桿	120
桁架	其他構件	150
柱及壓桿	主要的	120
柱及壓桿	次要的（牆骨、通風頂的支柱、檩條等）	150
聯結系	所有構件	200

受拉構件的長細比 λ，為其結合點或支承點間的長度 l 與其截面的最小旋幅 γ 的比。

受拉構件的長細比不得超過表十四的規定。

受拉構件的容許長細比　　　　　表十四

結構名稱	構件類別	最大長細比	
		直接受動力載	受靜力載
桁架	弦桿及與支承點結合的各桿	250	400
桁架	其他構件	350	400
聯結系	所有構件(拉條除外)	400	400

Steel Structure Design Standards and Technical Specifications

Contemporary

Paper

1/32

76 pages

In order to meet the needs of construction and structural design, the Technical Department of the State Ministry of Construction and Engineering at the time presided over the translation of the Soviet Union's Steel Structure Design Standards and Technical Specifications in 1956. However, since some provisions must be combined with China's specific conditions, they were not used as formal design specifications, but only for reference.

This book was translated by Cheng Jida and Liu Dajiang, proofread by Cai Yiyan, approved by the Technical Department of the Ministry of Construction and Engineering, and published by China Industry Press in 1957. It is the first collection of Steel Structure Museum and donated by Professor Cai.

左页

2. 用在助熔剂下的自动焊接时，采用Св-08、Св-08А、Св-08Г、Св-08ГА和Св-15、Св-15Г号锰钢和高锰钢焊丝，并采用相应的助熔剂标号。所采用的焊丝应符合"建筑法规"第一卷第一篇第十章的要求（见附录I表3）。

附注：① 如有充分的根据时，焊接Ст.2、Ст.3和Ст.4钢质制成的承受静载荷的结构，可采用符合"建筑法规"第一卷第一篇第十章要求的Э34型的焊條（附录I表3）。
② 对于铆接或栓接车间的冶金工厂的吊车梁间结构物中的車梁和桁架以及焊接直接承受辗行作业的梁的結构时，应采用：
甲，若手工焊接时，用Э42A型的焊條；
乙，若在助熔剂下用自动或半自动焊接时，应采用Св-08ГА号焊結和АН-348А、ОСЦ-45号的助熔剂或其他質量相当的曲焊剂。

第11条(2.6)　铆钉应使用符合"建筑法规"第一卷第一篇第十章要求的Ст.2和Ст.3号铆钉用的平炉热轧炭素钢和НЛ1号的低合金钢制作（见附录I表1）。

第12条(2.7)　螺栓应使用符合"建筑法规"第一卷第一篇第十章要求的Ст.3、Ст.5号普通質量炭素钢或НЛ1和НЛ2号低合金钢制作（见附录I表1）。

粗紋螺栓是使用符合"建筑法规"第一卷第一篇第十章要求的Ст.2和Ст.3号铆钉用的普通質量炭素钢制作（见附录I表1）。

附注：如有充分的根据时，螺栓可用Ст.0号钢制作。

第三章　材料和联結的标准指标

第13条(3.1)　辊轧钢（厚度4～40公厘）的匀質系数和标准强度，可分别按表1(1)的规定采用。

第14条(3.2)　炭素钢铸件的匀質系数和标准强度，应按表2(2)的规定采用。

右页

辊轧钢的匀質系数（K）和标准强度R^H
（公斤/平方公分）　　　　表1(1)

项次	标准指标	符号	Ст.0	Ст.2	Ст.3、Ст.4	Ст.5	НЛ1	НЛ2
			а	б	в	г	д	е
1	抗拉强度、抗压强度、抗弯强度	R^{H}_{u}	1,900	2,200	2,400	2,800	3,000	3,400
2	抗剪强度	R^{H}_{cp}	1,150	1,300	1,450	1,650	1,800	2,050
3	端面承压强度	$R^{H}_{cм.т}$	2,850	3,300	3,600	4,200	4,500	5,100
4	局部挤压承压强度	$R^{H}_{cм.м}$	1,450	1,650	1,800	2,200	2,250	2,550
5	混凝土自由抛擲物的撑的销层强度	$R^{H}_{c.к}$	70	80	90	105	110	125
6	匀質系数	k	0.9	0.9	0.9	0.85	0.85	0.85

炭素钢铸件的匀質系数K和标准强度R^H
（公斤/平方公分）　　　　表2(2)

项次	标准指标	符号	15Л	35Л
			а	б
1	抗拉强度、抗压强度、抗弯强度	R^{H}_{u}	2,000	2,800
2	抗剪强度	R^{H}_{cp}	1,200	1,700
3	端面承压强度	$R^{H}_{cм.т}$	3,000	4,200
4	局部挤压承压强度	$R^{H}_{cм.м}$	1,500	2,100
5	混凝土自由抛擲物的撑的销层强度	$R^{H}_{c.к}$	60	80
6	匀質系数	k	0.75	0.75

Steel Designers' Manual (English)

Contemporary

Paper

1/16

1092 pages

Published in 1955, this book was written by Charles S. Gray, technical advisor of the British Constructional Steelwork Association, and others. It aimed to bridge the gap between general design theory textbooks and the practical application of architectural engineering at that time, introduced advanced design methods applied to modern structures, and used examples as an important part. Most of the relevant data were given in tabular form. The compilation of the manual had been supported by the British Steel Manufacturers Conference and the British Iron and Steel Federation.

It is donated by the Chinese National Engineering Research Centre for Steel Construction (Hong Kong Branch).

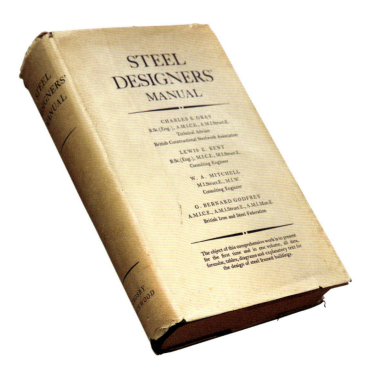

STEEL DESIGNERS' MANUAL

CHARLES S. GRAY
B.Sc.(Eng.), A.M.I.C.E., A.M.I.Struct.E.
Technical Adviser
British Constructional Steelwork Association

LEWIS E. KENT
B.Sc.(Eng.), M.I.C.E., M.I.Struct.E.
Consulting Engineer

W. A. MITCHELL
M.I.Struct.E., M.I.W.
Consulting Engineer

G. BERNARD GODFREY
A.M.I.C.E., A.M.I.Struct.E., A.M.I.Mun.E.
British Iron and Steel Federation

The object of this comprehensive work is to present for the first time and in one volume, all data, formulae, tables, diagrams and explanatory text for the design of steel framed buildings.

RIGID FRAME FORMULAS
by *A. Kleinlogel*

Professor Kleinlogel's famous book has been revised and enlarged so that it is now more useful and time saving than ever to the structural engineer. Now available for the first time in English, this handbook of reliable, compact formulas is an invaluable tool for every engineering office.
Illustrated 75/- net

BEAM FORMULAS
by *A. Kleinlogel*. Translated and revised by *Harold G. Lorsch*

An indispensable auxiliary to Kleinlogel's well-known *Rigid Frame Formulas*, this volume may also be used independently for the computation of simply supported beams. It contains more than seventy loading conditions covering the entire range of loads that occur in practical engineering. In addition, it presents formulas for general types of loads. An invaluable aid to engineers and designers, it saves hours of computation for statically determinate and indeterminate structures.
Illustrated 40/- net

STRUCTURAL THEORY AND DESIGN
ONE VOLUME EDITION
by *J. McHardy Young*, B.Sc. M.I.Struct.E. A.M.I.C.E.

'Covers a wide range of theory from the study of materials and the design of simple beams to the deflection of frames, and part of the subject matter is devoted to the design of reinforced concrete. The book is profusely illustrated and each chapter ends with a series of examples selected from Associate Membership Examinations. There are most informative chapters on the analysis and design of building frames, earth pressure, soil mechanics, foundations, etc. The author is to be congratulated on the general layout and the clarity and simplicity of the diagrams and illustrations.' STRUCTURAL ENGINEER. 30/- net

BUILDING AND CIVIL ENGINEERING PLANT
Spence Geddes, E. S. Diplomate, R.T.C. Glasgow

The correct application and efficient operation of plant requires considerable experience gained on works of construction, carrying out those operations on which plant can be employed. The object of this work is to make available a comprehensive book of reference on Building and Civil Engineering Plant so as to make possible a considered approach to its purchase and to ensure its correct application and efficient operation in carrying out the work. It is suitable for the Buyer, the Agent, the Site Engineer, the Plant Manager and all who are interested in plant and its efficient operation.
Illustrated throughout with half-tone photographs, line drawings and diagrams. 80/- net

CROSBY LOCKWOOD AND SON LTD
26 OLD BROMPTON ROAD, LONDON, S.W.7

Grashof's formulæ have been shown by experiment to be approximately correct for values of L/B exceeding 2, but when the plate is square, i.e. $L/B=1$, the stress is underestimated by 28 per cent. The reasons for the discrepancy in the case of approximately square plates may be demonstrated by reference to Fig. 299. Consider the central strip ab which is the most heavily stressed and will therefore govern the design of the plate. If this narrow strip, which is of unit width, were completely isolated from the re-

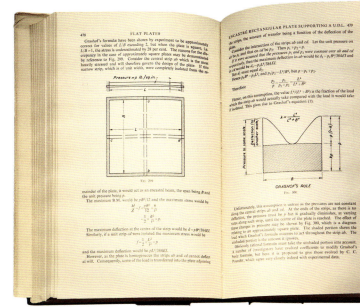

Fig. 299

mainder of the plate, it would act as an encastré beam, the span being B and the unit pressure being p.

The maximum B.M. would be $pB^2/12$ and the maximum stress would be

$$\frac{M}{Z} = f = \frac{pB^2}{12}\cdot\frac{6}{t^2}$$
$$= \frac{1}{2}\cdot\frac{B^2}{t^2}\cdot p.$$

The maximum deflection at the centre of the strip would be $d = pB^4/384EI$.

Similarly, if a unit strip cd were isolated the maximum stress would be

$$f = \frac{1}{2}\cdot\frac{L^2}{t^2}\cdot p$$

and the maximum deflection would be $pL^4/384EI$.

However, as the plate is homogeneous the strips ab and cd cannot deflect at will. Consequently, some of the load is transferred into the plate adjoining

the strip, the amount of transfer being a function of the deflection of the plate.

Consider the intersection of the strips ab and cd. Let the unit pressure on ab be p_1 and that on cd be p_2. Then $p_1 + p_2 = p$.

If it were assumed that the pressures p_1 and p_2 were constant over ab and cd respectively, then the maximum deflection in ab would be $d_1 = p_1B^4/384EI$ and in cd would be $d_2 = p_2L^4/384EI$.

But d_1 must equal d_2.

Hence $p_1B^4 = p_2L^4$, but $p = p_1 + p_2$.

Therefore

$$\frac{p_2}{p} = \frac{p_1}{p_1+p_2} = \frac{L^4}{L^4+B^4}$$

Hence, on this assumption, the value $L^4/(L^4+B^4)$ is the fraction of the load which the strip ab would actually take compared with the load it would take if isolated. This gives rise to Grashof's equation (1).

GRASHOF'S RULE
Fig. 300

Unfortunately, this assumption is untrue as the pressures are not constant along the central strips ab and cd. At the ends of the strips, as there is no deflection, the pressure must be p but it gradually diminishes, at varying rates along each strip, until the centre of the plate is reached. The effect of these changes in pressure may be shown by Fig. 300, which is a diagram relating to an approximately square plate. The shaded portion shows the load which Grashof's formula assumes to act throughout the strip ab. The unshaded portion is the amount it ignores.

Obviously rational formulæ must take the unshaded portion into account. A number of investigators have evolved coefficients to modify Grashof's basic formula, but here it is proposed to give those evolved by C. C. Pounder, which agree very closely indeed with experimental data.

People's Daily of October 16, 1957

Contemporary

Paper

Vertical: 52 cm

Horizontal: 38 cm

Wuhan Yangtze River Bridge, the first bridge over the ten-thousand-li river, was officially opened to traffic on October 15, 1957. This news was reported on the front page of the *People's Daily* published the next day under the heading "The train is flying across the Yangtze River-the millennium dream has become a reality, and everyone is happy with it".

It is donated by Ms. Xia Liying.

人民日报

1948年6月15日创刊 · 第3386号 · 地址 北京王府井大街117号

1957年10月
16
星期三
丁酉八月二十三

今日天气预报（北京地区）

上图：长江大桥全景

火车飞驰过长

千年理想成为现实 万众欢腾庆

表彰苏联专家对长江大桥的创造性贡献

国务院授予西林同志感谢状

铁道部授予格列佐夫等九同志感谢状

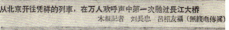

从北京开往凭祥的列车，在万人欢呼声中第一次驰过长江大桥

本报记者 刘长忠 吕相友摄（无线电传真）

汽车队伍浩浩荡荡通过长江大桥公路桥面

新华社记者 托纯一摄（无线电传真）

Wuhan Yangtze River Bridge

Contemporary

Paper

Length: 26 cm

Width: 18.5 cm

18 pages

This is a catalogue on the Wuhan Yangtze River Bridge, compiled by Wuhan Bridge Engineering Bureau, published by the Changjiang Literature and Art Publishing House and issued by the Xinhua Bookstore Wuhan Branch in October 1957. It has 18 pages in total and introduces details on the Bridge including the preparation and construction, a complete picture of the project, engineering data, new bridge foundation construction methods, the performance of the bridge builders, national support, and technical assistance from Soviet Union experts etc., illustrated with 21 photos and drawings.

It is donated by Ms. Tao Lei.

1957.10.

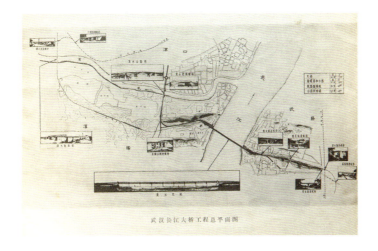

武汉长江大桥工程总面图

Building the Golden Gate Bridge: A Workers' Oral History (English)

Contemporary

Paper

1/32

195 pages

    This book is written by Harvey Schwartz and published by the University of Washington Press in 2015. It includes six chapters: overview of the Golden Gate Bridge, interviews with construction workers in San Francisco, interviews with steel structure workers, biography of construction workers, biography of steel structure workers, and biography of San Francisco.

    It is donated by Mr. Li Renge.

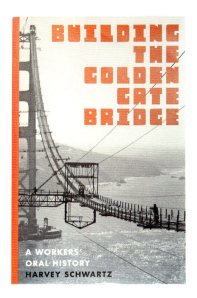

top of the tower. Other guys would go down. For the toilets on top, they had a cable so they could hook up about four of 'em at a time. They had a crane on top of the tower that you could use to hoist about anything you wanted up there. To clean them, they'd just drop 'em down. They cleaned 'em right there, right over into the bay. In those days, they weren't particular. When the toilets was cleaned up, they'd send 'em back up again.

When we was working on the cables, the only thing that stopped us was the wind. We worked rain or shine. When it was raining working for Roebling, we wore raincoats. But if the wind come up it would catch the wheel, which was about four feet in diameter, and turn it and the wire would jump off. Then we went home. You were paid for only the time you worked, too. Later, when I worked for Bethlehem, we didn't go to work on a job when it was storming. But like I said, just the wind is all that stopped us with Roebling. They wanted that cable in. They got it under their time limit, too.[12]

Roebling give us a big compliment after that. They told us we were the best bunch of ironworkers, and that they put more wire in every day than on any other jobs they'd ever worked. So we had a feather in our cap there. They give us a party up at Paradise Cove, too, that was a doozer. They took us up there by boat. There was all you could eat and all you could drink. They had barbecued steaks. Everything was really good. All the big shots were there, but there was very little speeches. There was no hanky-panky, either; it was just a party. When it was all over, they brought us back on the boat. There was no bonus. Instead, they give us that party and everybody was happy. I guess a lot of 'em had never seen anything like that. It was the first party I'd ever seen like that, so I was quite impressed with it.[13]

After my Roebling cable job is when I went to work for Bethlehem. First I worked down on the pier, on the bottom of the bridge where they had a dock built right there where the caisson was. Bethlehem used to bring the steel for the bridge roadway over from Alameda on a barge. It had come by ship for Bethlehem from Pennsylvania. It was all fabricated there and off-loaded in Alameda at the yard there. However rotation this iron

Workers using a cable squeezing machine, Golden Gate Bridge, 1936. After spinning was finished, the main cables were compressed into their final shape. Photo by Ted Huggins. Courtesy of California Historical Society, Huggins Collection, CHS Huggins.041.

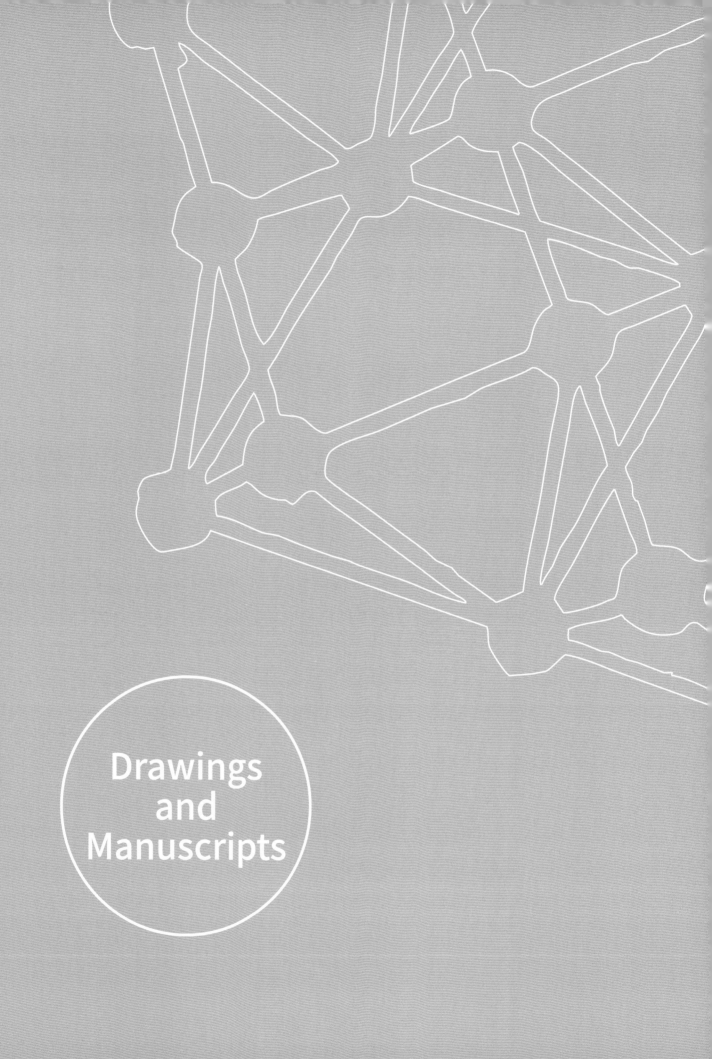

Drawings
and
Manuscripts

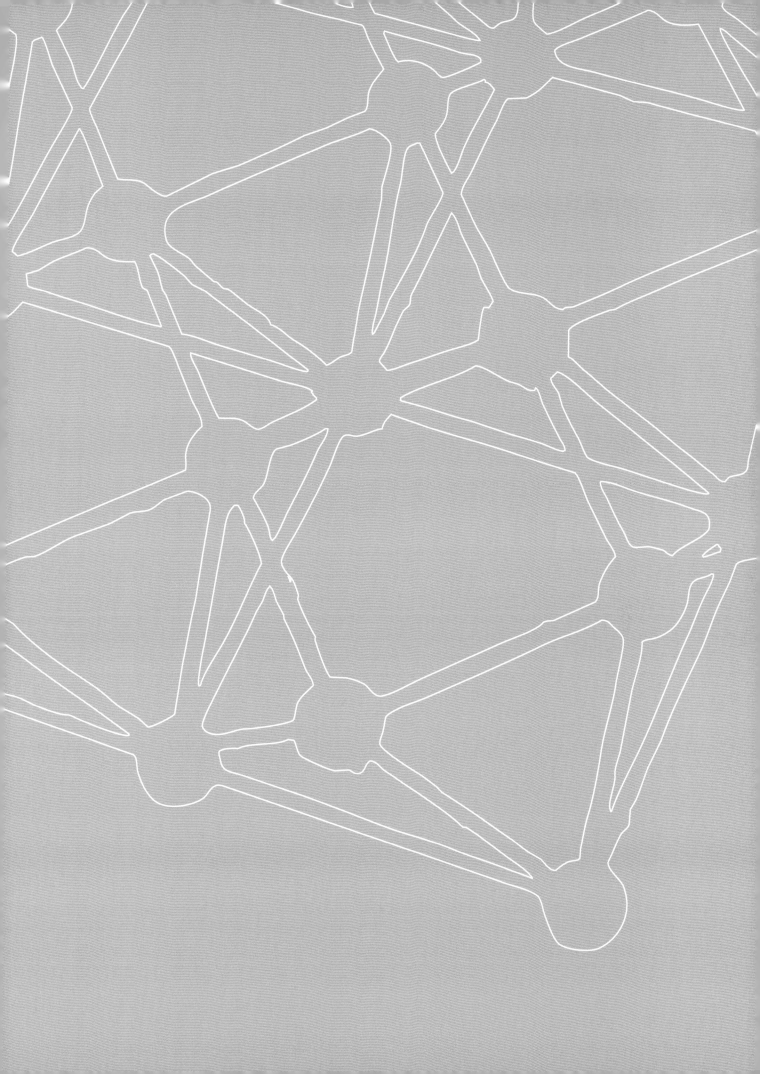

Recommendation Letter of *History of Wuhan Bridge Projects* (replica)

Modern

Paper

Vertical: 30 cm

Horizontal: 21 cm

This is a replica of the recommendation letter of *History of Wuhan Bridge Projects*, which was issued by the Central Plain Interim Government and presented to the Ministry of Railways of the Central Government in March 1949. To a certain extent, this manuscript witnessed the contribution of bridge pioneer Mr. Li Wenji and the planning and construction of Wuhan Bridge.

It is copied from Hubei Provincial Archives.

漢口市參議會 (8/)

批示	說明	擬辦	事由

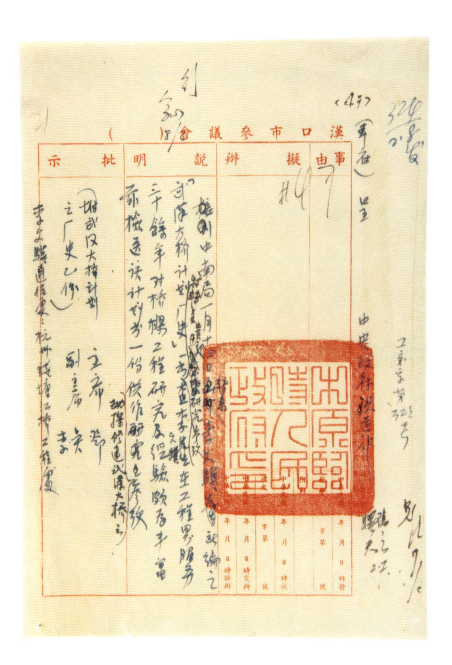

（附武漢兩大橋計劃
之「史乙作」）

李文驥通信處：杭州錢塘江橋工程處

Design Drawings of the Bank of China HK Branch (replica)

Contemporary

Paper

Vertical: 1 m

Horizontal: 0.9 m

The Bank of China Tower, abbreviated the BOC Tower, is one of the most recognizable skyscrapers in Hong Kong. It is located at 1 Garden Road and houses the headquarters of the Bank of China (Hong Kong) Limited.

Once the tallest building in Asia, this skyrise was designed by the world renowned Chinese-American architect I.M. Pei. It is covered in silver reflective glass making the structure a sight to behold whether at daytime or at night, when the city is aglow with all sorts of artificial light.

This is a replica of BOC Tower design plan, donated by the Chinese National Engineering Research Centre for Steel Construction (Hong Kong Branch).

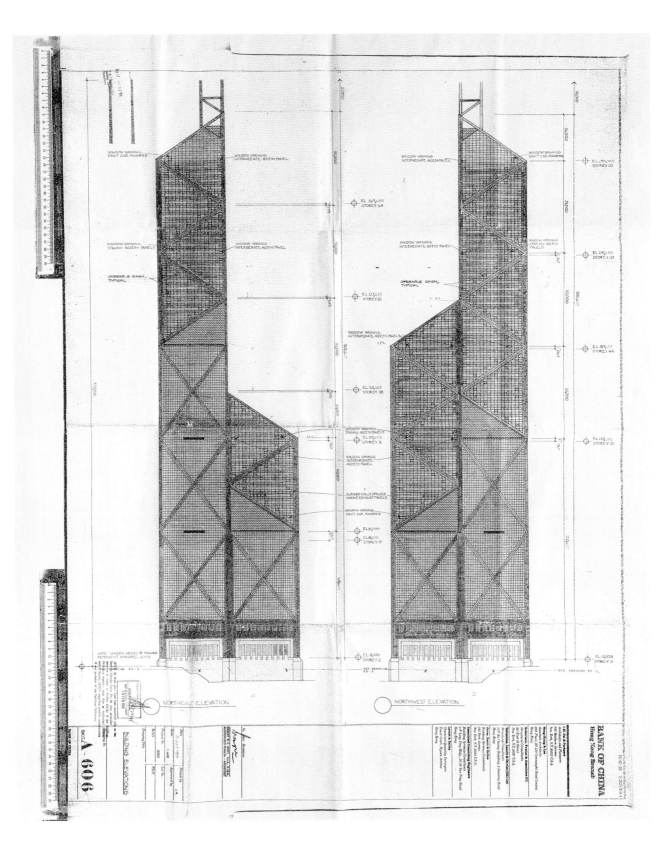

NORTHEAST ELEVATION

NORTHWEST ELEVATION

BANK OF CHINA
Hong Kong Branch

BUILDING ELEVATIONS

A-606

Postals,
Paper Notes
and Souvenir

Ten Dollar Note with Dr. Sun's Memorial Hall

Modern

Paper

Length: 16 cm

Width: 10 cm

This ten dollar note was issued by Guangzhou Municipal Bank in 1933. The middle picture on the front is the famous steel structure—Dr. Sun Yat-sen's Memorial Hall, and the back is the portrait of Dr. Sun. It is unique among Republic of China banknotes because of the horizontal English words on its back.

It is donated by Mr. Zhang Kaiming.

Postcard: Jintang Bridge Tianjin

Modern
Paper
Length: 15 cm
Width: 10 cm

The Jintang Bridge is located on the Haihe River in Tianjin, with a length of 76.4 meters and a total width of 10.5 meters. Originally built in 1906, it is one of the earliest large-scale steel bridges in existence in Tianjin and is currently the only rotary-opening steel bridge in China. Its joint constructors included Tianjin Custom Administration, Austrian and Italian Concessions, and Tianjin Electric Light Company. It was named Jintang Bridge, which means "very solid".

It is donated by Mr. Zhang Kaiming.

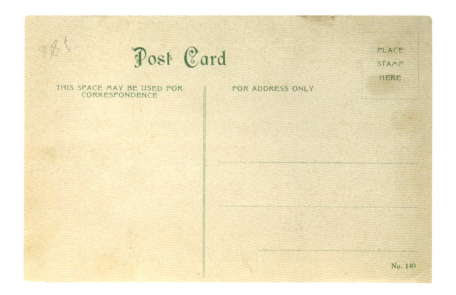

Tientsin, Austrian Bridge
Tientsin, Oesterreichische Brücke

Commemorative Envelope: Expo 67

Contemporary

Paper

Length: 16 cm

Width: 9 cm

This commemorative envelope was issued on May 25, 1967.

The theme of the Montreal World Expo (Expo 67) was Man and His World. A total of 62 countries participated in the event, which was a gift from the thriving Canada to the world, and an unprecedented success in the 100 year history of the World Expo. In 1967, the population of Canada was about 21 million, while the number of visitors to the Montreal World Expo exceeded 50 million. Such widespread public participation was unimaginable until now.

The monumental building printed on the envelope is the American Pavilion of Expo 67-known as the geodesic dome and designed by American architect, systems theorist, author, designer, inventor, and futurist Richard Buckminster Fuller. The triangular metal structure was reasonably combined into a sphere, which reached 76 meters in diameter. The building was like a delicate and beautiful crystal ball, shining in daylight and brightly lit at night.

It is donated by Mr. Zhang Lifeng.

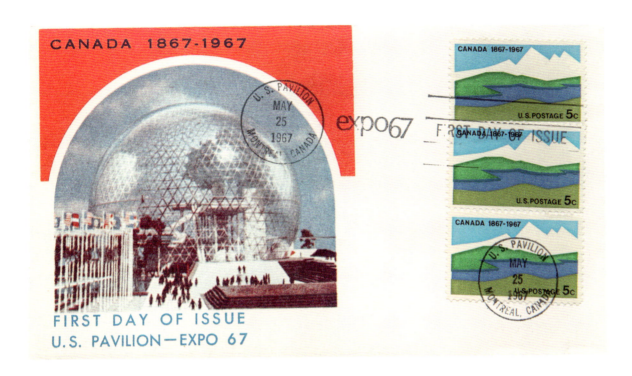

Medal for Closure of Nanjing Yangtze River Bridge Structure

Contemporary

Aluminum

Length: 3 cm

Width: 1.2 cm

Weight: 1.5 g

This aluminum medal was manufactured to commemorate the closure of Nanjing Yangtze River Bridge's main structure. The main colors of its front side are gold, red, and white, with Chairman Mao Zedong's portrait, the bridge's image, and a word "self-reliance" printed on it. Its back side is gold-colored and engraved a slogan "The closure of Nanjing Yangtze River Bridge's main structure is a great victory of Mao Zedong Thought".

The construction of Nanjing Yangtze River Bridge officially started on January 18, 1960, and the entire process was full of twists and turns. As for steel structures, the Soviet Union refused to supply steel shortly after the project started, due to the breakdown of Sino-Soviet relations. After hard research, Ansteel successfully developed the "16 Mn" steel that met the requirements. Thereafter, 14,000 tons of this type of steel were produced, which ensured the smooth progress of the project. In November 1966, erection of the main steel bridge started from both sides, until they got folded at Pier 4 on August 16, 1967.

It is donated by Mr. Zhang Kaiming.

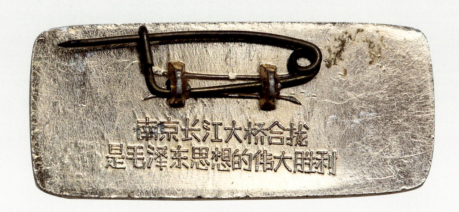

Postcard: Zhongshan Bridge Lanzhou (2)

Contemporary

Paper

Length: 15 cm

Width: 10 cm

These are postcards themed Zhongshan Bridge in Lanzhou and donated by Mr. Zhang Kaiming.

Zhongshan Bridge is commonly known as the Zhongshan Iron Bridge or the Yellow River Iron Bridge. It is the first truly fixed bridge on the Yellow River and opened to traffic in 1909. This 234-meter-long and 7.5-meter-wide bridge is a typical steel structure bridge, whose body adopts a freely supported riveted steel truss structure, with an arc-shaped steel frame beam placed above. It has a total of 4 piers and 5 spans. In memory of Dr. Sun Yat-sen, it was renamed Zhongshan Bridge in 1928. In 2006, this century-old bridge was listed one of the national key cultural relics by the National Cultural Heritage Administration.

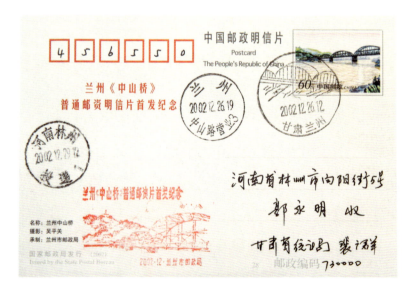

2002(2800)-0096

Commemorative Envelope: Reopen of Waibaidu Bridge

Contemporary

Paper

Length: 22 cm

Width: 12 cm

After 10-month repair, the hundred-year-old Waibaidu Bridge returned to its original state on February 26, 2009 and celebrated a reopening and lighting ceremony on April 10. A total of 20,100 "commemorative envelopes for the reopening and lighting of the Waibaidu Bridge" were issued on site. This is one of them.

It is donated by Mr. Xu Ziming.

Postcard: Jiefang Bridge Tianjin

Contemporary

Paper

Length: 15 cm

Width: 10 cm

Jiefang (Liberation) Bridge is a two-leaf vertical-open steel bridge with a length of 98 meters and deck width of 19.5 meters, located on the Haihe River between Tianjin Railway Station (East Station) and Jiefang North Road. It was completed in 1927 and originally called the Wanguo Bridge because of the concession territories of 9 foreign countries in Tianjin. People also called it the French Bridge since it was located at the entrance of the French concession territory and built under the auspices of the Concession's Industry and Construction Bureau. After the victory of the Sino-Japanese War, the National Government named it the Zhongzheng Bridge after Mr. Chiang Kai-shek. After the liberation of Tianjin in 1949, it was officially renamed Jiefang Bridge, which is still in use today.

It is donated by Ms. Wang Juan.

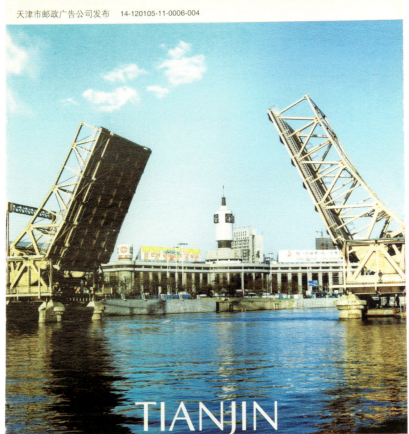

TIANJIN

天津·解放桥

Commemorative Envelope: Haizhu Bridge

Contemporary

Paper

Length: 22.5 cm

Width: 12 cm

Built in 1933, Haizhu Bridge is the first bridge across the Pearl River in Guangzhou and originally a simple-supported steel truss bridge. It has been repaired several times since its completion, as in 1995 the bridge became a self-anchored suspension bridge. It was overhauled again and resumed operation on September 1, 2013. The Philatelic Association of Haizhu District issued 2000 theme envelopes to commemorate this event.

It is collected from Guangzhou Municipal Archives.

163412

广州海珠桥大修竣工通车

2013.8

广州海珠桥修复通车
广东·广州2013年8-10月

广州
2013.09.01.22
江南大道15

中国邮政
￥000.70
粤AA352

黑龙江省大庆市银浪村5-2-32信箱

支 玉 杰 老师收

印 刷 品
IMPRIMES

广州苏村大道000号政政森新子江南邮   邮政编码   510000

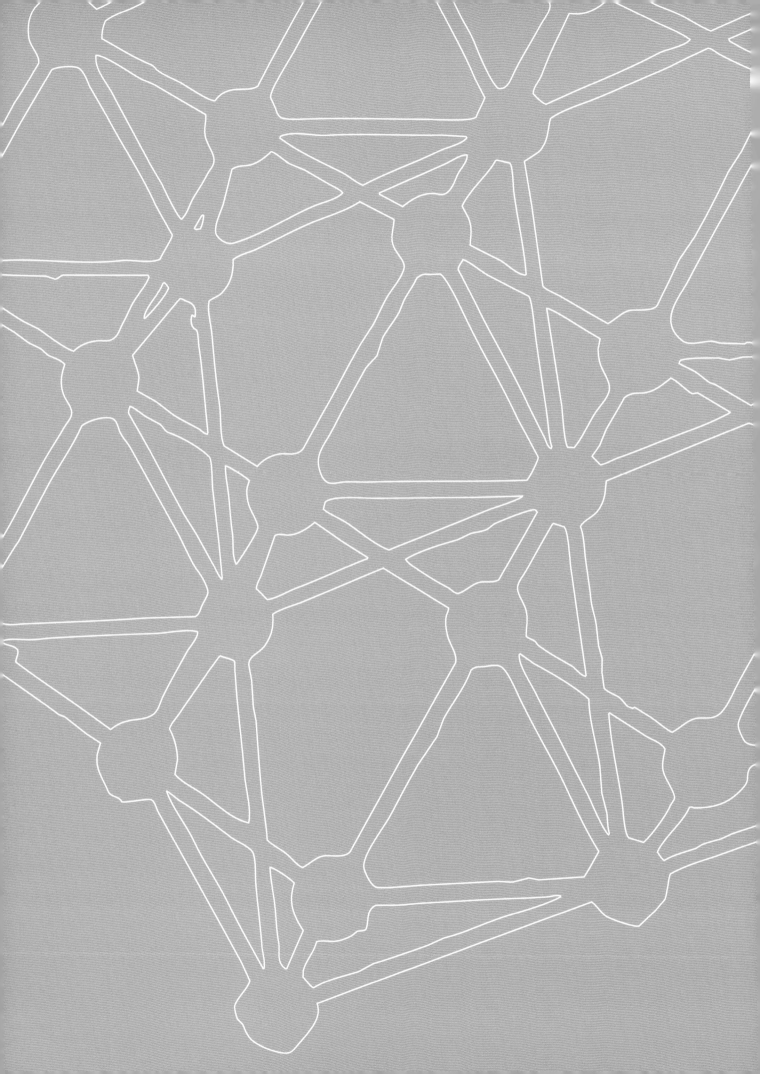

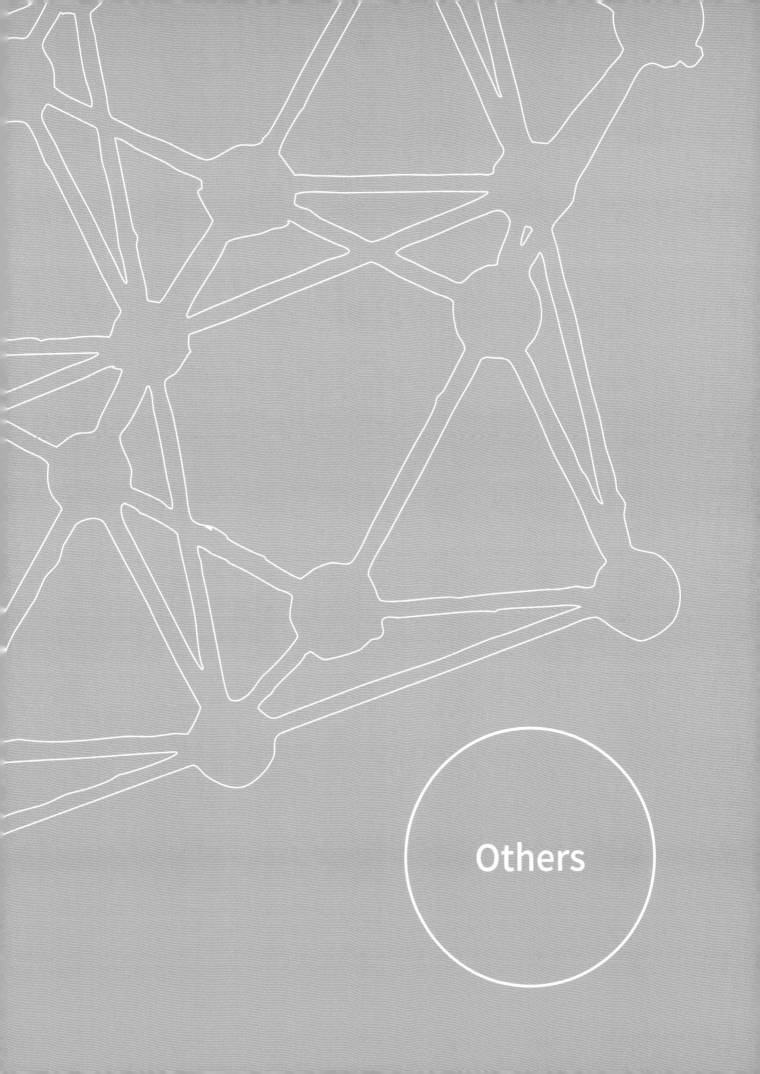

Others

Track of Peking-Kalgan Railway (partial)

Modern

Steel

Length: 56.5 cm

Gross width: 11 cm

Height: 13 cm

Weight: 25 kg

The Peking-Kalgan Railway is the first railway designed and built by the Chinese, as Mr. Zhan Tianyou served as the chief engineer. Its construction began in September 1905, and it was officially opened to traffic in 1909. The entire line started from Fengtai Liucun and passed Guangou to Zhangjiakou Station. Its total length is 201.2 kilometers, along which a total of 14 stations, 4 tunnels and 125 bridges were built, including 121 steel bridges.

This partial track of the Peking-Kalgan Railway, engraved with "K.T.P.E.R.S.W. 1909 V.", was manufactured in 1909 and donated by the Zhangjiakou Dept., Beijing Railway Bureau.

Plane Iron

Modern

Steel

Length: 8.5 cm

Width: 5.5 cm

Thickness: 0.7 cm

Weight: 200 g

Planing is a simple method common in traditional construction and manufacturing fields for processing planes and grooves with the tool planer.

The plane iron is the main component of the planer. This plane iron is a domestically produced article in the period of the Puppet Manchurian period, which was engraved with the words "shanlin" and "guaranteed use". It is purchased from folk collector.

It is donated by Mr. Zhang Kaiming.

Vise

Modern

Steel

Gross length: 7.5 cm

Gross width: 2 cm

Gross height: 10.5 cm

Weight: 300 g

A vise or vice is a mechanical apparatus used to secure an object to allow work to be performed on it. Vises have two parallel jaws, one fixed and the other movable, threaded in and out by a screw and lever.

It is donated by Mr. Zhang Kaiming.

Chronicles of Showa Steel Works (Japanese)

Modern

Paper

1/16

422 pages

This chronicles, as an internal reading material not available for sale, was edited by Showa Steel Works in 1940.

Showa Steel Works, the predecessor of the Ansteel, was established by Japanese invaders and dated back to the early 20th century. In 1909, Japanese invaders illegally explored eight iron mines in Anshan and seized the mining rights. Then in 1933, with the support of the Ministry of Military Affairs, the Japanese government relocated the Showa Steel Plant originally set in North Korea to Anshan, and built a steel plant on the basis of the existing Anshan Iron Plant. They subsequently became a steel complex, who achieved it highest production capacity in 1943.

With a total of 422 pages and about 100,000 words, this book records not only the development history of the Japanese steel industry in detail, but also the evidence of the Japanese robbery, which is of great historical significance.

It is donated by Mr. Liu Jinzhang.

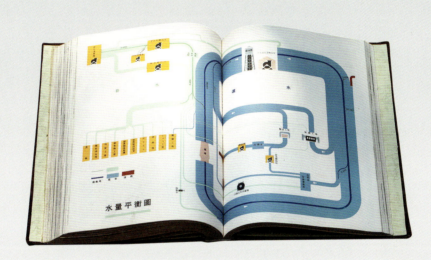

水量平衡圖

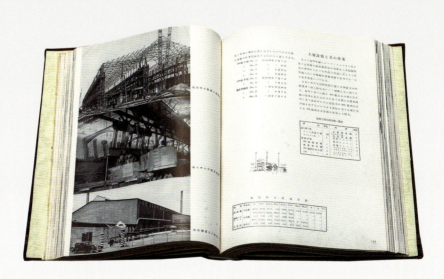